George -
Happy Valentine's Day   1976
          Love, Gertrude

MODERN MILITARY SERIES
WARSHIPS

MODERN MILITARY SERIES
Editor Michael Leitch

WARSHIPS

by H. P. Willmott
Introduction by Aram Bakshian, Jr

Octopus Books

First published 1975 by Octopus Books Limited
59 Grosvenor Street, London W1

ISBN 0 7064 0356 8
© 1975 Octopus Books Limited

Produced by Mandarin Publishers Limited
Westlands Road, Quarry Bay, Hong Kong
Printed in Hong Kong

JACKET FRONT *A bird's eye view of an American warship's secondary and tertiary armament.*

JACKET BACK *The American polaris submarine Abraham Lincoln caught in the evening sunlight.*

PAGE 1 *HMS Warspite another nuclear-powered submarine wallows whale-like in the North Sea.*

PREVIOUS PAGES *A moment of relaxation on the main deck of the USS Arkansas on patrol in World War II.*

THIS PAGE *The French warship Richelieu cleared for action (1944).*

Contents

Introduction

by Aram Bakshian, Jr

Too often, perhaps, the dramatic focal point of wars has been located on land rather than at sea. More schoolboy imaginations over the years have surely been fired by tales of Waterloo or Gettysburg or El Alamein than by the oceanic struggles that were fought on the fringes of each great war – often with far more decisive results. Edmund Waller's poetic vision of an England 'guarded with ships, and all our sea our own', became a serious goal of later statesmen and it was this supremacy, more than any land-locked battle, that led to the downfall of both Napoleon and the Kaiser. The overwhelming naval superiority of the North in the American Civil War was equally instrumental in isolating and starving the Confederacy into submission. Indeed, there are those who maintain that the Civil War could have been settled with a far smaller loss of life if the North had placed more initial reliance on its strength at sea and avoided some of the bloody, indecisive land battles of the war's opening phase.

Throughout the 19th and 20th centuries, a strong fleet has been the mark of every major power seeking a position of ascendancy, and naval defeats have often symbolized the decline of the once great. The triumph of the Japanese over the decaying naval might of Imperial Russia at the turn of the century was an omen of things to come, and the massive naval build-up of the Soviet Union today, at a time when most Western powers are cutting back on naval strength, has been witnessed with grave foreboding by many military experts for the same reason. Mastery of the Mediterranean by one of the great land powers of Europe –

a goal that neither Louis XIV nor Napoleon could achieve – may ultimately be realized by the modern heirs of the Romanovs.

Meanwhile, in the absence and continuing unlikelihood of a Third World War, national fleets remain an important part of diplomacy, as witnessed by American deployments of naval task forces in Indochinese, Indian and Middle Eastern waters during moments of crisis in recent years. An entirely new aspect of naval strength, the creation of nuclear-armed and -powered submarines, has also made the ocean depths a new theatre of potential war and a murky haven for weapons of destruction capable of wiping out whole cities thousands of miles away.

H. P. Willmott's *Warships*, a valuable addition to the Octopus Modern Military Series, tells the story of modern warships and modern naval warfare in an informative and comprehensive text. Like the other titles in the series, *Warships* will take a welcome place on the bookshelf of many a modeller, illustrator and military history buff. Even considered from its most technical angles this story of ocean warriors is of intense human interest for, as Admiral Samuel Eliot Morrison, one of the greatest of modern naval historians, has written: 'The nations that have enjoyed sea power even for a brief period – Athens, Scandinavia, the Netherlands, England, the United States – are those that have preserved freedom for themselves and have given it to others.'

One hopes that what has been true through past millennia will remain so as mankind enters its 21st century.

OPPOSITE *Part of the British Mediterranean fleet at anchor in Malta harbour.*

Chapter One

Sea Power: From Galley to Ironclad

Sea power is the means by which a nation contests, secures and maintains a command of the sea sufficient to allow it to transport economic and military resources at will whilst denying such facilities to an enemy. This power is built on several distinct foundations, e.g. bases, dockyards, ordnance factories and the merchant marine; but in many people's minds sea power is identified more particularly with the warship.

Yet if the warship has a certain symbolic value, this is clearly a secondary function. What, then, are the primary or 'real' tasks of the warship? What strategic and tactical aims does it fulfil?

Essentially, the strategic and tactical concepts of every nation are determined by the most powerful weapon of destruction in existence at any given time; and the nature of the weapon itself is dictated by the level of technical sophistication at that time. Warships, which are a compromise between armament, defence, the power that drives them and the material they are made of, reflect the technological situation at any given moment. They are, moreover, built either directly around the most powerful weapon of destruction or in support of the ship that carries it.

In 1815 the only type of fighting ship was one built around a crude and inaccurate cannon. Armed with broadsides of smooth-bore muzzle-loading cannon and moved by wind and tide, the wooden sailing ship had, from the latter part of the 16th century onwards, largely taken over from the galley (and its immediate successor, the galleass) as the principal naval unit.

The galley had dominated the waters of the Mediterranean for centuries. It was light yet strong and possessed powers of independent movement – achieved through its banks of oars – but little offensive power. Its ram was not a particularly effective weapon and there was but a fine distinction – measurable in terms of a few yards – between ramming and being rammed. Sea fighting was little more than an extension of land warfare. The main weapon was the boarding party with 'fire support' from arrows, lime, flame and stone. At this stage the skill of the mariner was subordinate to the command of the soldier. The galley

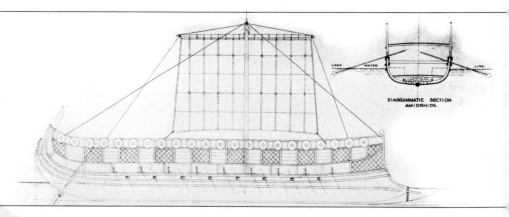

DIAGRAMMATIC SECTION AMIDSHIPS.

remained dominant until the cannon ceased to be a small, weak, anti-personnel weapon fit for use only against boarders and had developed into a heavy ordnance piece capable of inflicting serious damage on a ship.

Increasing weights of gun and shot could not be countered by the galley. Heavier gun carriages necessitated stronger decks; heavier shot needed thicker sides for defence; but the accumulation of weight would have robbed the galley of its two great advantages: speed and mobility. Unsuccessful attempts were made to incorporate guns on a galley (the galleass) but no satisfactory solution appeared until the power of independent movement – via the oars – was sacrificed in the cause of improved offensive power.

The gun demanded and obtained its own platform – the sailing ship. This type of vessel, unlike the short-ranged galley, possessed the power of virtually unlimited sea endurance. The sailing ship flourished along Europe's Atlantic seaboard where waters were rough and where the galley could not be as effective as it was in the generally calmer Mediterranean. Thus it was the northern European countries, particularly England, that largely pioneered the development of the gun-carrying sailing ship. Voyages of discovery and the acquisition of overseas empires accelerated the process and other European states followed this lead.

Even so, for much of the 16th century the galley/galleass and the sailing ship existed side by side. Indeed the galley survived almost until the 19th century in the calm and well-charted waters of the Black and Baltic Seas – though these were now backwaters, the balance of naval power having shifted elsewhere. In much the same way that many machines achieve the peak of their power just before their replacement by superior devices, the galley and the

ABOVE *Galleys and galleasses in conflict at the peak of their development, in the Battle of Lepanto, 1571.*

OPPOSITE *A new era dawns in naval warfare as the gunned sailing ships of England and Spain meet in their famous battle of 1588. The scene depicts the fighting off Gravelines, and shows the English fire-ships going into action.*

RIGHT *A 24-pounder cannon retrieved from the wreck of the Swedish warship Vasa, which sank in 1628.*

galleass reached their zenith at the Battle of Lepanto in 1571 – only 17 years before the gunned sailing ships of England and Spain fought their historic duel around the coasts of the British Isles.

Between 1588 and 1815 the development of the fighting ship was very slow. There was continual evolution as keel construction changed and ships grew in size and displacement, in complement, and in the number and size of their guns. Yet, fundamentally, Nelson's ships were little different from those of Drake, and the Englishmen who opposed the Armada could have manned the *Victory* with little difficulty; the skills of seamanship and gunnery had not changed. Since, too, knowledge of ship construction was universally the same, there was a marked similarity between the ships of different nations. However, within 50 years of Waterloo, the harmony of two and a half centuries of evolution was swept aside by the impact of the Industrial Revolution.

In the vanguard of change were the French. An impressive run of defeats had made them willing, indeed anxious, to consider new methods of construction and fighting that would challenge Britain's supremacy. All the nations followed France's lead – even Britain, though she tended to do so with reluctance, being loath to abandon systems that had served her well. As a result of this new surge of activity, the similarities in design that had existed collapsed as the paths of the nations gradually divided. Working with new materials and with new concepts on the very fringes of knowledge, designers now had no common pool of experience or guidance on which to draw. The results were individualistic, often bizarre, and occasionally disastrous.

The first technological change came in the field of propulsion. The steam engine was developed virtually simultaneously in Britain, France and the United States at the time of the French Revolutionary and Napoleonic Wars. Passenger-carrying steam ships seem to have been in use in the first decade of the 19th century and probably the first cargo-carrying steamer plied the Mississippi in 1811. During the War of 1812 the Americans, spurred by defeat and the pressures of a naval blockade, planned a double-keeled steam ship called the *Demologos* to contest the Royal Navy's command of the seas; but peace was signed before anything came of it. In 1815 the British carried out unsuccessful experiments with a converted ship, the *Congo*, but failed to pursue the work after early reverses. The first application of steam to the fighting navies came in a much humbler form and followed the lead of the merchant fleets, which used tugs to take ocean-going ships to sea against prevailing winds. The first steam ships in the Royal Navy were the tugs *Monkey* (1821), *Comet* (1822) and *Sprightly* (1823).

It was quickly realized that auxiliary steam propulsion would be of great value even in ocean-going ships, since it would avoid the problems of being becalmed and would also give some tactical as well as strategic mobility. But, initially, attempts to fit warships with steam power were unsuccessful, for at this time the paddle provided the method of movement and the placing amidships of paddles and engines led to a considerable reduction in gun power; independent movement had been regained – but at too great a price in offensive power. Eventually the screw propeller solved this problem: it was carried beneath the waterline and, unlike the paddle, was largely invulnerable to gunfire; moreover, the engines had to be carried lower in a screw ship than in a paddlewheeler, and so they had little adverse effect on gun space.

However, it took a long time for screw propulsion to gain widespread acceptance and it was not until 1850 that the first battleship designed with auxiliary screw power was laid down. In a sense this ship, the *Napoleon*, started the first technological naval race as France and Great Britain sought to out-build and out-convert one another. By 1858 there were 76 ships with auxiliary screw power, evenly divided between the two countries, but already the advantage lay slightly with the French who had, in 1855, announced a programme that totalled 40 battleships, 30 corvettes and 60 other craft. The British, on the other hand, had no long-term programme and were responding to events rather than imposing their will upon them.

The French programme was, however, cut short by developments in other fields. During the Crimean War (1853–6) the British and French fleets used their traditional type of ship with success against the Russians, but it

ABOVE *HMS* Victory, *Nelson's flagship; her design was little different from Drake's 16th-century warships.*
OPPOSITE *The launching in 1814 of the American double-keeled steam warship* Demologos. *The advent at this time of steam propulsion was the first of many technological changes.*
RIGHT *The* Napoleon, *laid down in 1850; this was the first battleship designed with auxiliary screw power.*
BELOW *The British tug* Monkey *(1821), the first steam ship in the Royal Navy.*

PREVIOUS PAGES *Steam leading sail. The 'Fighting Temeraire' is towed to her last berth, 1838; from the painting by Turner. Inset is the* Great Britain, *Brunel's revolutionary steamship.*
ABOVE La Gloire *(1858); a new type of ship, designed in France, its wooden hull was protected by iron.*
OPPOSITE, ABOVE *The* Devastation; *a predecessor of La Gloire, she served in Crimea with armour plating added to the hull.*
OPPOSITE, BELOW *The* Warrior, *the world's first iron warship.*

clearly emerged that the continued existence of such ships was gravely threatened by increasing offensive power. Shells had been used with devastating effect by the Russians against the Turkish fleet in November 1853 at the Battle of Sinope, an encounter that showed the vulnerability of wooden ships to explosive and incendiary shells.

The immediate answer to the shell was provided by the French. On 17 October 1855, during an attack on the fortress of Kinburn, the French used three naval batteries, those of the *Devastation*, the *Tonnante* and the *Lave*, with their main battle line. These craft had auxiliary steam power and carried 16 guns that fired 56-pounder shells. But, most

important of all, each ship had 4·5 inches of iron plating covering the basic 18 inches of wood that protected the ships. Between them the French ships took 134 hits but suffered no appreciable damage.

Armour seemed to offer an effective answer to the shell. But shells, too, were undergoing revolutionary changes, as were the methods used to fire them. Soon after the Crimean War it was appreciated that the cylinder made a more efficient projectile shape than the long-established sphere, and the cylinder was then generally adopted. This, coupled with the rifling of gun barrels – to impart spin and hence a better-controlled flight – promised greater accuracy as well as improved penetrative powers. In addition, improved breech mechanisms were appearing which made it likely that most guns would be breech-loaded in the foreseeable future; from a naval point of view, especially, this would considerably ease the problems of loading, since guns would not have to be run in for loading via their muzzles. All these developments appeared to augur a period when the offensive would take the ascendancy over the defence.

In 1858 the French, after some hesitation, laid down at

Toulon a new type of ship, a wooden-hulled but iron-protected frigate – *La Gloire*[1]. Three further ships were ordered, one of which was to have an iron hull. But the French were outbuilt by the British. As early as 1845, possibly influenced by Brunel's revolutionary steamship, the *Great Britain*,[2] the Admiralty had countenanced iron frigates, but had been prevented from taking such a step by outraged public reaction. Since that time, engines and boilers had improved and grown larger, so increasing the strain on the wooden parts of ships. The promise – or threat – of still bigger guns and the new onus of armour were burdens that wood could no longer take; by now it had reached the limit of its strength. Finally, on 29 December 1860, the *Warrior*, the world's first iron war ship, was launched and with her came a new era of ship construction.

[1] Although she had about twice the displacement of a battleship, she was classified as a frigate because her guns were laid out on a single deck.
[2] Brunel's remarkable ship was the first ocean-going ship to be built of iron, to have a clipper bow, screw propulsion and a balanced rudder – an impressive collection of 'firsts'.

Chapter Two

Warships of Iron

The *Warrior*, a frigate displacing over 9,200 tons, carried an armament of 26 68-pounder, 14 110-pounder and 4 70-pounder guns. Unlike *La Gloire*, which was armoured over the complete length of her waterline, the *Warrior* was unarmoured at bow and stern; her belt, 4·5 inches of wrought iron backed by 18 inches of teak, extended only over 56 per cent of her length. The ends were sealed by 4·5-inch bulkheads which thereby produced a citadel within which most of the guns were sited. The French, on the other hand, correctly appreciated that in future *all* guns would have to be behind armour; the *Magenta* and the *Solferino*, the only two-deck broadside ironclads ever built, carried all their 34 16-cm and 16 19-cm guns within the citadel.

The *Warrior* and the early French ships shared a common disability: though very strong defensively, they lacked the firepower to sink another ironclad warship. Rifling did not substantially aid that firepower, and the first breech-loaders anyway left much to be desired. Indeed, the *Warrior*'s 68-pounder muzzle-loading guns showed themselves to be superior to the others, which were all breech-loaders, with the result that the ship was subsequently re-armed solely with 68-pounders. Nevertheless, not even these guns could inflict damage on a scale that was likely to be decisive. To overcome the power of the defence, heavier and more powerful guns were needed.

The French attempted to solve this problem by the suppression of the broadside. The latter was, in fact, an inefficient method of arranging guns since it meant that the field of fire was mainly restricted to one at 90° to the ship's direction of travel. The broadside was suppressed in favour of fewer but heavier guns capable of firing through wide arcs. All of these 'pivotal' guns were positioned behind armour in what became known as a 'central battery'. The British followed and developed the French idea until the first years of the 1870s, by which time this type of arrangement was passing into obsolescence.

LEFT *The* Monitor, *a turreted steel-clad warship that fought on the Federal side in the American Civil War.*
TOP *The double-turreted US warship* Terror; *this was a retrograde design, being made of wood.*

The era of the central-battery ship coincided with the meteoric rise of the 'ram ship'; but this, like a meteor, faded from the scene almost as rapidly as it had arrived. In 1866, at the Battle of Lissa, the Austrian battleship *Ferdinand Max* had rammed and sunk the Italian battleship *Re d'Italia*. That the Italian ship had been previously crippled by gunfire and, furthermore, that this was the only occasion when a ship was successfully rammed in the course of a battle that abounded in such attempts, were factors brushed aside at the time as being of no account; and so the ram became established as a powerful offensive weapon. In the late 1860s ram ships were built by most navies, though it quickly became apparent that rams were much over-estimated. The chances of ramming a ship that still had full power of manoeuvre and adequate sea room were small, and the increasing power of artillery suggested that a ram ship would be unable to close to effective range, without herself being crippled.

Nevertheless, in the course of its short life, the ram ship helped to produce a successor to the central-battery idea. Ram ships carried little in the way of gun power, and what they had was generally sited over the bows. From this alternative pattern it was next recognized that all-round fire was desirable, and the *Hotspur*, laid down in 1868, in-corporated a turret. A moving turntable trained a single gun through four loopholes cut in fixed armour.

It seems that the turret was first patented in 1859 by Captain Cowper Coles, RN. His idea had sprung from an armoured raft that he had designed in 1855 as a result of combat experience in the Crimea. There he had constructed an armed raft that drew only 20 inches of water and was used for inshore bombardment. The turret could be incorporated in such craft, and in river gunboats, because in their design little store was set by seakeeping qualities. Designers of ocean-going craft had, on the other hand, to allow for the fact that the weight of a turret tended to reduce freeboard – the area between waterline and deck – to the detriment of seaworthiness. But this did not prevent Coles from designing a ship of 9,200 tons with 10 cupolas – the dome-shaped structures protecting the guns – and 20 breech-loaders. Not surprisingly the idea was rejected, but in 1861 the Admiralty carried out tests on turrets.

The turret showed unanticipated powers of resistance – and this was confirmed in the fight between the USS *Monitor* and the CSS *Merrimack* in Hampton Roads on 9 March 1862. The 10-gunned *Merrimack*'s easy successes gained against wooden Union ships (including the first successful ramming of a ship, the *Cumberland*, in modern

A scene from the historic six-hour engagement between Monitor *and the Confederate ship* Merrimac*; this battle established the virtues of the turreted fighting ship.*
ABOVE, RIGHT *The raft* Lady Nancy, *carrying a 32-pounder gun into shallow waters at Taganrog, Crimea. In the foreground is a whaler mounting a Congreve rocket launcher.*

times) were not repeated when the Confederate vessel engaged the 2-gunned, turreted *Monitor*. A six-hour engagement did no serious damage to either ship but the *Monitor*'s performance proved the obvious desirability of turrets; it was equally obvious that ships such as the *Monitor*, whose deck was only a few inches above the water, were not capable of anything but the most limited operations. Indeed, the *Monitor* was lost in the first gale she encountered in December 1862.

The first British turret ships were coastal defence craft, then in 1868 the launching took place of the first ocean-going ship with turrets, the *Monarch*. Able to make nearly

15 knots under steam and sail, the 8,300-ton *Monarch* carried four 12-inch guns in two central turrets. She was followed by the *Captain*, which carried the tallest and heaviest masts in the Royal Navy. She also had a very low freeboard of 8·5 feet which was further reduced as excess weight was worked into her during construction. The *Captain* soon foundered, in a gale that she should have survived. Her loss, on 6–7 September 1870, resulted in a temporary set-back for the turret but hastened the passing of masts and rigging. After the *Captain* only three British battleships carried a full rig, and steam emerged from being the auxiliary to become the only means of propulsion.

The 1860s was thus a confused era of shipbuilding with several different types of armament vying with each other for acceptance. But by the early years of the next decade the issues of steam and sail, turret, central battery and broadside had been largely resolved. In the 1870s the major developments centred around the monster gun. In 1872 the Italians laid down the *Duilio*, a battleship to be armed with four 12-inch 38-ton guns. During construction she was altered to take first 15-inch 50-ton guns and then 17·7-inch 100-ton guns. The continual modification of the initial design caused the Italians a variety of problems: ultimately the ship was so weakly armoured that she could

not have engaged any comparable ship with much hope of survival. Her huge guns were also so slow to work that the chances of hitting an enemy were rather slim. Nevertheless the *Duilio* was widely acclaimed and her effect was immediate. Other nations had to increase the size of their guns and the armour protection afforded their ships. The *Inflexible*, the British response, carried up to 24 inches of compound armour (iron backed by teak and steel) in her central areas while her waterline bulkheads were up to 22 inches thick. She also incorporated an armoured deck below the waterline and was extensively sub-divided in order to control flooding.

The era of the monster gun was, however, fairly short. The destructive potential of a 110-ton gun was formidable – on paper. In reality it was less impressive. Not only were the guns extremely slow to fire (the *Inflexible*, with one round every two minutes, was comparatively fast), they were also very inaccurate. As early as 1871, attention was drawn to the poor shooting of British ships: in one trial a carefully laid gun on HMS *Hotspur* missed the target (another battleship) at 200 yards' range in a flat calm, both target and firer being stationary.

One further problem arose at this time, that of whether the ships could take the strain caused by the prolonged firing of their own guns. There was obviously a need for ships with smaller and more numerous guns that would put down a heavy volume of fire rather than a few very heavy shots. From such a volume of fire, it was reckoned, there should be enough punishing hits to secure a lasting advantage without having to close to ranges at which even the monster guns, with their erratic record, would find it impossible to miss.

In the 1880s several major developments in gunnery took place, as a result of which, after extensive trials and many errors, the breech-loading gun was generally adopted in favour of the muzzle-loader. The new breech-loaders were lighter than earlier versions had been, and this prompted two design changes in the ships that carried them. Firstly, high freeboard was regained, and with it came immediate benefits in terms of speed and seaworthiness. Secondly, more guns could now be carried per ship, and battleships began to assume the design usually associated with modern warships in general and with battleships in particular: this incorporated a main armament in turrets fore and aft, with the intermediate and secondary armaments placed amidships between the heavy guns. The

OPPOSITE *The British ocean-going turret ship* Captain, *whose design was dangerously encumbered by incorporating the tallest, and heaviest, masts in the Royal Navy.*

ABOVE HMS Devastation, *a double-screw armour-plated turret ship built in 1871.*

RIGHT *The Italian battleship* Duilio, *whose armament was increased during construction from 12 to 17·7 inches; her* hitting *power so outstripped her armour that she could not have hoped to survive in combat with a comparably armed ship.*

BELOW *The British warship* HMS Sultan, *seen offshore during a trial run.*

Collingwood, launched in 1882 but not completed for another four and a half years, was the first British ship to adopt this general design – though her heavy guns were in unprotected barbettes and not turrets. The *Collingwood* was also the first British ship to carry her secondary and tertiary armaments grouped in batteries. By the time she entered service, a third development, the introduction of the Quick-Firing (QF) gun, was in the pipeline. The *Nile* and the *Trafalgar*, both laid down in 1886, were the first British ships to carry a QF secondary armament and within a short space of time even the heavy guns were capable of rapid fire.

The QF gun met a pressing need for the navies of the world. It provided a means of countering the first development to challenge the monopoly of the gun – the torpedo, and its delivery system, the torpedo boat.

Until the 1870s the word 'torpedo' described any underwater weapon; thereafter, as the search for such weapons intensified, the word came to embrace all weapons with the power of independent movement. They were thus distinguished from weapons that were either moored or moved by tide and current.

The idea of striking at a ship at its most vulnerable part – below the waterline – by means of an explosive charge may be traced back to the latter part of the 16th century, but it was not until the beginning of the 19th century that the prototype of the modern mine was developed. Robert Fulton, an American, invented an explosive charge contained in a metal case for action against ships; the charge was detonated by clockwork. The first major breakthrough in mine development came in 1843 when Samuel Colt, the

inventor of the revolver, devised a 'controlled' mine that was detonated by an electric current operated from an observation post ashore. A similar though separate development was made in Kiel at about the same time and weapons of this type were used in the defence of the harbour against the Danish fleet in the war of 1848.

Subsequently contact mines, designed to explode when in collision with a ship, came into being. A small gunpowder charge was detonated when the tubes protruding from the sides of the mine were broken by collision with their target. This brought sulphuric acid into contact with potassium chlorate and sugar which in turn generated enough heat and flame to set off the main charge.

Mines were extensively used by the Russians during the Crimean War but they caused no losses; the first ship lost to a mine was the USS *Cairo* in the Battle of Yazoo River on 12 December 1862. Mines were improved when a more efficient method of detonation was found, and a means of safely laying the mine to a prescribed depth. The British solved the latter problem by laying the mine with a sinker (or anchor) which dropped it to the seabed. The mine was automatically released once the laying ship was clear and then rose on a cable towards the surface. When it reached the level at which it was to operate, water pressure activated a hydrostat which in turn worked a brake on the cable. At that point the mine was armed and ready for action.

By the end of the 19th century the mine had developed into a formidable weapon. In the course of the Russo–Japanese War of 1904–5 – the first war in which it was used on an extensive scale – the Russians lost a battleship, a cruiser, two destroyers and two smaller craft to mines while the Japanese lost, to the same weapon, two battleships (their only battleship casualties), four cruisers, two destroyers, a torpedo boat and a minelayer. The war clearly showed the dangers facing any navy that tried to blockade an enemy coast. Although it could be laid with equal facility in the open sea or offensively in the enemy's home waters, the mine was seen, ideally, as a defensive weapon that protected a coastline and its harbours.

The 'locomotive' torpedo, sometimes called the 'fish' or 'Whitehead' torpedo, was developed in Fiume, Austria (later Trieste, Italy) in 1866. The men responsible were Captain Luppis of the Austrian Navy and Robert Whitehead, a Scottish engineer who collaborated with him and who later introduced an improved model. Not unnaturally, the first prototypes were erratic and poor performers: this was partly because they lacked adequate means of steering and depth-keeping. Measuring some 14 feet by 14 inches and weighing 300 pounds (of which only 18 pounds was warhead), these early torpedoes had a maximum range of about 370 yards at 6 knots. At this low speed avoiding action was not difficult and an attacker had to come virtually alongside his intended victim to be sure of a hit. But the range of the 'locomotive' torpedo was not as poor as those of its immediate rivals – the 'spar' and 'towed' torpedoes.

The 'spar' was an explosive charge carried on the end of a pole over the bows of a very fast attacker. It was detonated either by ramming it into the side of a victim or by lowering it under the keel and then activating the charge by pulling a string. It was by the former method that a Confederate hand-cranked submerged craft sank the Union sloop *Housatonic* on the night of 17 February 1864 – the first time a surface warship was sunk by an underwater craft (which was itself destroyed in the attempt).

The 'towed' torpedo was pulled by a very fast craft at an angle to its course across the bows or stern of the intended target. The latter, fouling the wire that held the torpedo, then in theory pulled the weapon onto itself. But, in reality, the 'towed' torpedo needed liberal assistance on the part of the victim if it was to be successful.

The 'locomotive' torpedo at least had the advantages over its rivals that it was capable of improvement and did not demand suicidal tendencies on the part of the user. It also outlived one further challenge, that of the 'Brennan' torpedo. This was a wire-guided torpedo developed in Australia in the 1880s. However, the mass of wire needed for long-range work was dangerous on board a ship, and so the 'Brennan' was used mainly from the shore.

The problems encountered by Whitehead's improved locomotive torpedo in maintaining a steady course and a set depth were gradually overcome. Contra-rotating propellers helped to steady a torpedo on its course, but it was not until the invention of the gyroscope in the mid-1890s that accuracy could be guaranteed; the horizontal rudder, developed in 1877, went some way to solve the problem of depth-keeping. But even without these refinements the torpedo was able to claim its first victim. On the night of 25–26 January 1878 the Russian ships *Tchesma* and *Sulina* sank the 2,000-ton Turkish guardship *Intikbah* in Batum harbour – though they had to close to less than 80 yards.

But, in general, the growing size and range of torpedoes made it possible to attack with greater safety. By the beginning of the 1890s the torpedo had a 300-pound warhead and a range of over 1,000 yards at 30 knots, and it was possible to launch the weapon from below the waterline of a moving ship.

BELOW *Japanese picquet boats in the Russo-Japanese War, rigged for dropping mines off Port Arthur.*

The development of the torpedo gave a much-needed boost to the morale of submarine pioneers, for, unlike its predecessors, it did not entail immediate danger to the attacker. Furthermore, the submarine, by attacking under water, would avoid the heavy fire that any surface ship would have to face in view of the torpedo's restricted range. However, the technical limitations of the day kept the submarine as still merely an ideal. The same horizontal rudder that aided the development of the torpedo substantially helped to control the dive of a submarine but there was no safe and reliable means of propulsion, either on the surface or submerged. Steam propulsion was not suitable to a vessel that had to dive (though *Le Plongeur*, a French craft built in 1863, was able to travel considerable distances underwater with her fires banked and using the head of steam that had been built up). Neither at the time was there any means of accurate underwater navigation, nor had any really suitable material been found for building submarines. Thus the proponents of torpedo warfare were forced in the early years to use surface craft as the means of launching the new weapon.

The first torpedo boats were built in the mid-1870s by France and Russia; both countries appreciated the potential for threatening British naval supremacy with the new weapon and its launching craft. The first torpedo boats were small and not particularly seaworthy, consisting of little more than boilers and engines encased in a lightweight hull. Everything was sacrificed to high speed. The ships had a limited range and no accommodation and their crews soon proved unable to cope with their tasks in poor

weather conditions. It was quickly seen that such craft could not operate offensively on the high seas.

An alternative did exist, however. This was to take the torpedo boats with the fleet on-board other, larger ships. Thus for a while small, 20-ton torpedo craft were carried to the scene of an action, there to engage the enemy. (How then to recover them, in the face of the enemy, seems to have been an unresolved problem.) The Royal Navy built one such carrier, the *Vulcan*: launched in 1889, she carried six small torpedo boats; but by then it was already clear that she and her like could never be more than a short-term expedient. The real solution lay in heavier, more seaworthy torpedo boats that were greater in both speed and range.

So the torpedo boat began to increase in size. The first Russian versions, which appeared in 1877, were only 75 feet × 10 feet – allegedly small enough to be moved between the Baltic and Black Seas by rail. But in the same year the British built a 90-foot ship capable of 19 knots – a speed that earned her the name *Lightning*.

As these new ships emerged from the dockyards, there naturally arose a need for a ship to counter them. After 1885 the British responded by laying down 'catchers'. These were designed to be more seaworthy and more heavily gunned than their intended prey, but unfortunately their low speed rendered them of dubious value. By the beginning of the 1890s the 'catchers' were in fact slower than torpedo boats only a quarter their size. Nor was the Quick-Firing secondary armament of the heavy ships adequate to the task of destroying the torpedo boats. Some form of new craft was obviously required.

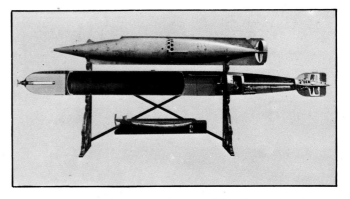

ABOVE *Three torpedoes: from the top, a 16-inch torpedo of 1870; a cutaway of a 14-incher fitted with a gyroscope, and a model of Captain Luppi's first locomotive torpedo, 1867.*
BELOW *Fitting an electro-contact mine aboard HMS* Vernon.

Chapter Three
The Coming of Steel

Between 1890 and 1914 there was a period of relative stability in ship design. Many important changes and developments took place but mainly these were evolutionary rather than revolutionary in character. This period also marked an end to the era of rapid advances that had produced ships of widely differing characteristics and power and prevented the building up of homogeneous squadrons.

The new continuity that was being achieved was most marked in the battleship. In December 1893 the British laid down the first of the *Majestics*, a new class. The basic design of this class was to be followed until 1900, by which time 29 ships had been laid down. The *Majestics* benefited from the introduction of Harvey steel armour and the new wire-wound 12-inch gun: considerable savings in weight were thereby effected for no loss of power. The compound armour of earlier classes was halved with no loss to the

RIGHT *HMS* Majestic, *laid down in 1893, was armed with four 12-inch and twelve 6-inch guns, whereas the USS* Kentucky *(opposite, above) had an intermediate (8-inch) gun in the main armament, which in total comprised four 13-inch, eight 8-inch and four 6-inch guns.*

defence; turrets enclosed the new guns whilst 6-inch casements defended the 6-inch armament. Throughout the citadel, armour was a uniform 9 inches thick, with a 14-inch bulkhead forward. A 2·5-inch curved protective deck ran from the citadel to the extremities. This basic design was improved upon by successors though the essentials were retained. Thus the later *Canopus* class ships were fitted with improved Krupp steel armour and the new water-tube boilers, which gave them a 2-knot advantage over the *Majestics*. And the *Formidable* class, laid down in 1898, incorporated the new 12-inch 40-calibre gun, which fired a

smaller shell than the older 35-calibre weapon of the *Majestics* but had a much higher muzzle velocity and greater powers of penetration.

The first major British departure from the *Majestic* type of layout came with the *King Edward VII* class. This was brought about as a result of pressure exerted by overseas designs. On ships of similar displacement, the British found the ships of other nations carried greater armament. Whereas the *Majestic* class carried four 12-inch and 12 6-inch guns in the main armament (with 16 12-pounder and 12 3-pounder guns for anti-torpedo boat work), the USS *Oregon*, laid down two years before the first *Majestic*, carried an intermediate gun in the main armament. She carried four 13-inch, eight 8-inch and four 6-inch guns, while the later *Kentucky* had four 13-inch, four 8-inch and 14 5-inch guns in the main armament. Italian ships also carried three types of gun in the main armament, but with them a more important factor was their high speed. Seeking to take advantage of their country's central position in the Mediterranean – and very conscious of the exposed nature of her long coasts – the Italians placed great store by the strategic and tactical mobility conferred by very high speed. (It was a policy which they were to continue until World War II). The *Sardegna* of 1893 and the *Vittorio Emanuele* of 1907 could make over 20 knots – though this was obtained at the expense of armour protection.

The *King Edward VII* class brought the British into line with these more powerful ships. They carried four 12-inch, four 9·2-inch and 10 6-inch guns in the main armament; however, this arrangement was heavily attacked. Its opponents felt that there were too many types and too few guns, and that the 6-inch guns could have been suppressed in favour of more 9·2-inch guns. The latter was much more powerful than the 6-inch and only a little slower in its rate of fire. With the *Lord Nelson* class, laid down in 1905, this alternative arrangement was tried. The two ships of this class carried four 12-inch and 10 9·2-inch

HMS Dreadnought (1906)

This design, using all big guns in the main armament revolutionized the appearance of battleships; after her, battleships in service were divided into categories of pre- and post-dreadnought. The diagram (opposite, top) shows the *Dreadnought's* gun layout: five twin turrets, two mounted *en echelon*, carried her twelve 12-inch guns.

SPECIFICATIONS

Displacement	17,900 tons
Length	527 feet
Beam	82 feet
Draught	26 feet 6 inches
Armament	10 12-inch guns
	27 12-pounders
	5 18-inch torpedo tubes
Main armour	11-4 inch belt
Engines	23,000 hp; turbines
Speed	21 knots

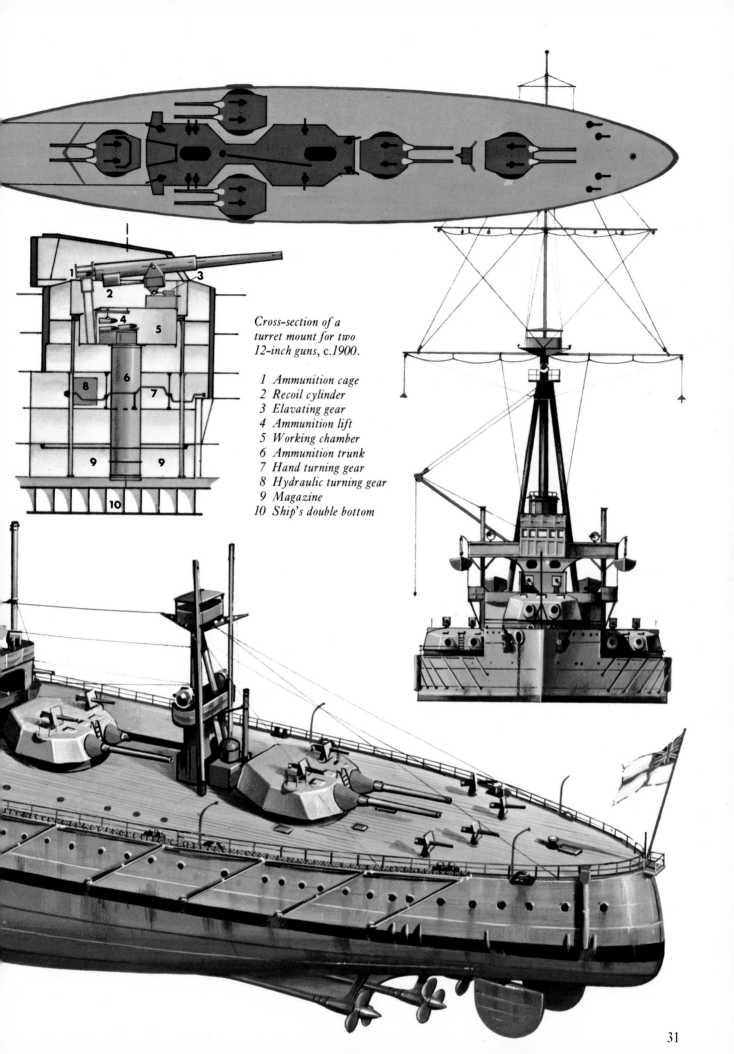

Cross-section of a
turret mount for two
12-inch guns, c.1900.

1 Ammunition cage
2 Recoil cylinder
3 Elavating gear
4 Ammunition lift
5 Working chamber
6 Ammunition trunk
7 Hand turning gear
8 Hydraulic turning gear
9 Magazine
10 Ship's double bottom

guns and were the last British ships to carry a mixed primary armament. Even before these ships were laid down it was suggested within the Admiralty that the main armament should be 12 12-inch guns, but the idea was rejected.

That same year (1905) the concept of a uniform heavy armament was accepted independently in the USA and Britain. This happened for two reasons. Firstly, the effectiveness of light and medium weapons was increasingly questioned; only the heaviest guns seemed likely to inflict damage upon a well-defended battleship. Thus there was an inducement to arm battleships with the heaviest guns available. Secondly, a uniform heavy armament simplified the problems of fire control. Uniformity of guns ensured a uniform flight time for shells firing to the same range. It was now possible to carry out salvo firing in order to estimate range – correction being made after observers had noted the fall of shot.

This procedure had become essential because the development of the torpedo had brought an end to close-range actions. At the turn of the century the accepted battle range was still about 1,000 yards, for although by that time the torpedo had grown in size and speed, it had not greatly improved in range and accuracy. But by 1905 the 18-inch torpedo had a range of 4,000 yards at 19 knots or a speed of 33 knots over 1,000 yards. Accuracy had been improved and new methods of propulsion had been developed. There was obviously a need for ships to be able to fight at longer ranges.

The result was the *Dreadnought*, a ship whose name became a universal description for ships of her type. With her armament of 10 12-inch guns, she completely outclassed any other battleship; the fighting value of every other mixed-armament battleship, either built or being built, was drastically reduced. It was seen that henceforward the first nation to acquire its own squadrons of dreadnoughts would be very powerfully placed to secure command of the sea. In the subsequent race to build up dreadnought fleets, the British had the priceless advantage of being first in the field, which gave them a one-year lead over other nations. In addition they possessed superior building facilities, but this did not prevent serious challenges from emerging – particularly from Germany.

Between 1905 and 1914 nine nations built and commissioned dreadnoughts and four other nations programmed this type of ship. During that time considerable improvements were made and the ships' dimensions and gun power

The defeat of the Russian fleet in the war against Japan was a humiliating blow.
BELOW *The battleship* Pobeda, *lost on 22 December 1904.*
OPPOSITE, ABOVE *The* Mikasa, *flagship of Admiral Togo at the great Japanese victory of Tsushima, 27–28 May 1905.*
OPPOSITE, BELOW *A Russian light cruiser fires on the enemy during the defence of Port Arthur.*

were continually increased. The *Dreadnought*, on a 17,900-ton displacement, carried five twin turrets; but broadside fire was limited to eight guns because two turrets were carried *en echelon*. This system of mounting guns was followed by the Germans, the French and the Japanese; other nations, not among the first to lay down dreadnoughts, followed the American system of all-centre-line guns. But few followed the superimposed arrangement that the Americans introduced into their first dreadnoughts, the *South Carolina* and the *Michigan*. In these ships the Americans developed the classically simple outline of battleship that was later adopted by all nations.

This arrangement made possible much smaller dimensions: the *Michigan* was nearly 40 feet smaller than the *Dreadnought* and displaced only 16,000 tons, but she had the same broadside. She also had one turret fewer, which was also a great saving given that speed of construction was governed not by shipbuilding facilities but by ordnance capacity. The British did not lay down an all-centre-line/superimposed battleship until the *Orion* of November 1909. This ship also marked the first increase in gun size carried out by the British.

While most navies adopted the 12-inch gun for their first dreadnoughts, the Germans chose the slightly inferior 11-inch gun. In 1908 they came into line and this in part prompted the British to adopt, in 1909, the 13·5-inch gun. The same process was followed by all navies: the Japanese, after one class of 12-inch guns, moved up to 14-inch guns with the *Fuso*, which was laid down in March 1912; and the French increased to a 13·4-inch gun after producing only the *Paris* class.

The Americans worked on the number of guns rather than their size. They built five entire classes carrying 12-inch guns before the 14-inch gun was adopted in the *New York* class of 1911. In that time, too, the length of US dreadnoughts had grown from the 452 feet 9 inches of the *South Carolina* to the 562 feet of the *Wyoming*. The latter, a 26,000-ton ship, was able, moreover, to carry 12 12-inch guns.

During this period turret arrangements also changed. Before 1914 the British never broke faith with the twin turret, whereas in 1909 the Russians and Italians incorporated the triple turret in their first dreadnoughts. This lead was followed by Austria–Hungary in 1910 and by the Americans in the *Oklahoma* class, laid down in 1912. In 1913 the French projected the *Normandie* class, whose ships were to have carried 12 13·4-inch guns in three quadruple turrets; but the ships were never completed.

The seeming disadvantage of the British in terms of numbers of guns per turret was offset by a superior number of ships and by the greater size of those ships. The last and most important change before World War I was the adoption of the 15-inch gun in the *Queen Elizabeth* class, whose ships also had the distinction of being the first battleships to dispense with coal in favour of oil. In many ways these ships were classics of their time, for they were faster and more heavily armed than any other battleship in the world – and as well protected. Yet such power was obtained only at a price. The 25,800 tons of the previous class had increased to over 29,000 tons, whilst engine capacity had almost trebled. In 1911 the *Iron Duke* class made 21 knots with 29,000 horsepower; the new battleships, specially designed to be a fast squadron of 25 knots, needed 75,000 hp to achieve their best speed of 24 knots.

Earlier, while the *Dreadnought* was being programmed, three ships of a new type were laid down. These were battle-cruisers, which had the armament of a battleship and the speed and protection of a cruiser. They were intended to act as a fast battle-squadron that could scout for and support the battleships as well as hunt down enemy commerce-raiders (fighting ships which attacked merchantmen). Only the Germans and Japanese followed with their own battlecruisers.

Initially the battlecruiser was smaller and less powerful than the battleship. The *Invincible*, the first of the type, displaced 17,250 tons and carried eight 12-inch guns, six of which could be fired on the broadside. Armour was very thin with only a 6-inch belt and 7 inches of armour over the turrets and barbettes. She was designed for 25 knots but proved capable of over 28 knots. This speed, however, could not disguise the fact that she could not take punishment of the kind she was able to inflict. German battlecruisers, on the other hand, were far better equipped defensively. The *Von der Tann*, Germany's first battlecruiser, had a 9·75-inch belt, and all her eight 11-inch guns could be trained on either broadside. The battlecruisers were subject to exactly the same increases in size and power as the battleships, but the demand for higher speed was often the critical factor. In 1912 the *Lion*, laid down in 1909, became the first warship to cost more than £2 million and the first battlecruiser to exceed the proportions of her battleship contemporaries: whereas the battleship *Thunderer* displaced 22,500 tons and cost £1,885,000, the *Lion* displaced 26,350 tons and cost £201,000 more.

The spiral of cost and size continued to rise. The *Tiger*, laid down in 1912, displaced 28,500 tons and cost nearly £2,600,000. She was Britain's last capital ship to use coal (at full speed she exhausted her bunkers in three days) and she was also the only British battlecruiser to carry a 6-inch secondary armament.

By introducing the 6-inch gun into the secondary armament, the British gave belated recognition to the increased power of the torpedo and the increased size of the destroyer. In terms of passive defence against the improved torpedo, anti-torpedo nets were needed and also armoured double-bottomed keels with the outer bottom sub-divided longitudinally and transversely. In the 1890s the French introduced a partially successful semi-circular bulkhead, whilst the Russians tried armoured bulkheads backed by bunkers. Extensive sub-division was worked into all heavy ships after 1905.

But while it was desirable to contain damage, it was obviously more important to avoid it in the first place if possible. High speed was one counter but better still was an increased anti-torpedo-boat armament that would keep the attacker outside effective range. At the turn of the century the 12-pounder gun was quite adequate to deal with the small craft then in existence. The battlecruiser *Invincible* was given 4-inch guns but for many years the British resisted logic and refused to adopt a heavier weapon in spite of the diminishing effectiveness of this weapon. The Japanese were better prepared, clearly as a result of their war experiences; initially, the 6-inch gun was their main secondary weapon, but this was later followed by the handier 5·5-inch gun. The Americans introduced the 5-inch gun into their second dreadnought programme, and the Germans had their 5·9-inch gun.

Like other types of ship the torpedo boat and the destroyer also grew in size and performance during this period. From

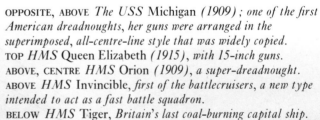

OPPOSITE, ABOVE *The USS* Michigan *(1909)*; *one of the first American dreadnoughts, her guns were arranged in the superimposed, all-centre-line style that was widely copied.*
TOP *HMS* Queen Elizabeth *(1915), with 15-inch guns.*
ABOVE, CENTRE *HMS* Orion *(1909), a super-dreadnought.*
ABOVE *HMS* Invincible, *first of the battlecruisers, a new type intended to act as a fast battle squadron.*
BELOW *HMS* Tiger, *Britain's last coal-burning capital ship.*

1908 onwards the Royal Navy, the emphasis of its tactical doctrine now placed on defence, discontinued building the relatively lightweight torpedo boats and concentrated on building destroyers capable of defending the battle line. The Germans, on the other hand, were wedded to an offensive concept and built destroyers that lacked the heavy-gun armament of the British ships but carried a greater torpedo armament. German destroyers, initially called large torpedo boats, were built for the first time in 1899 and carried three 4-pounder guns and three 18-inch tubes. One of the chief characteristics of German destroyers was their high forecastles, which made them very seaworthy and gave a good speed in bad weather. The early British destroyers were turtle-decked, and this meant that their speed quickly fell away in rough conditions. When the high forecastle was introduced in 1903 in the *River* class, the increase in weight caused speed to be reduced to 26 knots from the very high speeds that had been obtained with the steam turbines of the *Viper*. Launched in 1899, the latter had been designed for 31 knots but at trials she made 36·8 knots. Unfortunately she was subsequently wrecked and another destroyer with turbines, the *Cobra*, was also lost: these two losses checked the introduction of the turbine into widespread service for several years.

The first class to be given turbines was the *Tribal*: launched between 1907 and 1909, these were also the first ships to burn oil instead of coal. The first ships of the class were given three 12-pounder guns but the later ships carried two 4-inch 25-pounder guns. British ships lacked uniformity, however, for the builders were allowed great freedom within certain limits. It was not until the *Basilisk* (1909) and *Acorn* (1911) classes that standardization was achieved.

German destroyers showed greater uniformity: partly this was because only three dockyards built destroyers. Turbines were first incorporated in the *S-125* (launched in May 1904) and used in every class after 1909. The Germans did not abandon coal until quite late in the day: ships of the *U-25* class, the first of which was launched in January 1914, were the first to carry oil and no coal. The Americans were moving at approximately the same pace. After an initial class of 16 ships, no destroyers were built between 1902 and 1909 but thereafter the *Smith* class was given turbines and the subsequent *Pauldings* were oil-burners. These craft were well-gunned but a little slow by European standards.

By the outbreak of war in 1914 the destroyer was only one of three means of delivering torpedoes. The latest

ABOVE *A newcomer to naval warfare was the airship, intended for reconnaissance and bombing duties. Shown here is the Zeppelin L-1, which was delivered to the German Navy in 1912.*
BELOW *A German torpedo boat destroyer, 1901.*
OPPOSITE *The first aerial torpedo launch, made one week before the Great War began by a Short floatplane of the Royal Naval Air Service.*

method was achieved just one week before Britain declared war on Germany. At Calshot, on 28 July, an especially lightened Short aircraft of the Royal Naval Air Service launched a 14-inch 800-pound torpedo from the air. Even though the torpedo was small compared to those carried by destroyers, it was still a remarkable performance in view of the fact that the first controlled flight did not take place until 1903.

The aircraft that launched this torpedo was a seaplane, just one of four types of flying device competing for the limited funds available for air research and development at the time. The seaplane's immediate rival was the land-based wheeled aircraft. The balance between them was close. The seaplane had a slower rate of climb, inferior mobility and a lower ceiling than the other, but it could carry a radio and it could be recovered at sea. Both types had a very limited endurance and small bomb loads, which made them inferior to airships.

There were two types of airship – the non-rigid and the rigid (or Zeppelin). Of the latter, more formidable type, the German version was superior in quality to those of other nations. In 1909 the Zeppelin LZ-5 was accepted by the German Army after a 24-hour endurance flight, during which time she cruised 820 miles. This provoked British imitation in the form of Naval Airship No. 1, which failed to live up to her nickname, the 'Mayfly'. Then in 1912 the German Navy took delivery of its first Zeppelin, the L-1. This craft had a 47-knot speed and a lifting capacity of 9·25 tons. Within a year the L-3 had proved its endurance capabilities; this craft, moreover, could carry a bomb load of 1,000 pounds.

The non-rigid airship lacked the very long range and the relatively heavy payload of the rigid type but it was much smaller and needed only one-third of the crew carried by a Zeppelin. The chief weaknesses of the rigid airship were that very large numbers of men were needed to man and service the craft, and also that moving them into and from their mooring sheds in blustery conditions proved to be a dangerous exercise. When war broke out, Britain had seven airships of different types compared to Germany's single Zeppelin.

The final means of delivering the torpedo was the submarine, which had been developed at the turn of the century. The previously insoluble problems that had thwarted submarine development – the lack of a suitable building material, a safe method of propulsion and an accurate method of navigation – had been overcome. Steel, light yet strong, proved the ideal material; the invention of the internal combustion engine provided a means of surface propulsion whilst the development of the accumulator battery gave a means of underwater movement. Finally, the gyrocompass promised to overcome the problem of accurate navigation when submerged; the first submarine to have such a compass carried it on the outside of the hull where it was observed through glass.

By 1900 six navies had 10 submarines between them. The French had been the pioneers of the new craft and they had had no small success with it, but the decisive breakthrough came in the United States. An American submarine, the *Holland*, named after its Irish inventor, became the prototype for most of the world's navies (only the Germans and French remained aloof). The *Holland* displaced 105 tons and had a surface speed of 8·5 knots. Her hull was divided into three compartments which housed the engine, control and torpedo rooms. Under the latter two were tank and battery space. She carried a single bow tube. The British, who for years had tried to discourage the development of such craft, secured the plans and built their own submarine, the *A-1*. This was superior to the *Holland* in that it incorporated a periscope and a conning tower, both of which the *Holland* lacked.

The British and French quickly pulled ahead of other nations in the number of submarines they had in commission. In 1914 Britain had 75 and France 67, but many

of these were old and their strength in modern, long-range submarines was no greater than that of Germany, which had only 30 U-boats (Unterseeboote). Germany started building submarines in 1906 and from the start incorporated double-hulls and twin-screws in all boats. Unlike the British, who had started with petrol engines, the Germans initially installed heavy oil engines until 1908, when they introduced diesel engines. After their first major programme of 1907, the Germans concentrated on large 'overseas' boats. The *U-19*, completed in 1913, had a 4,000-mile range and a diving depth of 275 feet. The British were a little

not only outpaced that of possible antidotes to it but also any systematic consideration of how submarines might best be used. For political and humanitarian reasons, nations were unwilling to accept the idea that submarines would be used primarily against commerce. It was generally assumed that this form of war would be conducted by cruisers.

Traditionally, cruisers had fulfilled two roles: on the one hand they scouted for the battle fleet and on the other they protected or preyed on commerce. Because iron came, first of all, to battleships, the cruiser then suffered an eclipse from which it did not emerge for many years. In those early

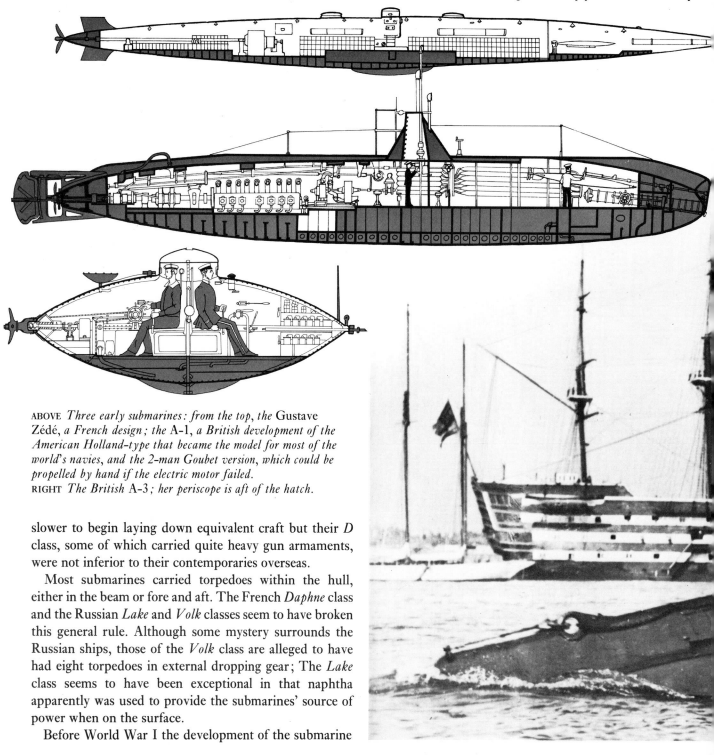

ABOVE *Three early submarines: from the top, the* Gustave Zédé, *a French design; the* A-1, *a British development of the American Holland-type that became the model for most of the world's navies, and the 2-man Goubet version, which could be propelled by hand if the electric motor failed.*
RIGHT *The British* A-3; *her periscope is aft of the hatch.*

slower to begin laying down equivalent craft but their *D* class, some of which carried quite heavy gun armaments, were not inferior to their contemporaries overseas.

Most submarines carried torpedoes within the hull, either in the beam or fore and aft. The French *Daphne* class and the Russian *Lake* and *Volk* classes seem to have broken this general rule. Although some mystery surrounds the Russian ships, those of the *Volk* class are alleged to have had eight torpedoes in external dropping gear; The *Lake* class seems to have been exceptional in that naphtha apparently was used to provide the submarines' source of power when on the surface.

Before World War I the development of the submarine

years, not surprisingly, the wooden cruiser could neither run away from nor stand up to the iron battleship. Later, when iron and then steel were used in the construction of cruisers, there was no agreement over what constituted a proper balance between high speed, long range and gun-power. As a result the cruiser, in the period between 1870 and 1890, went through the same sort of uncertain phase as had befallen the early iron battleships – a phase marked by continued experimentation at the expense of continuity and uniformity.

The first iron cruiser was the British *Inconstant*, which was almost as large as contemporary battleships. Her high cost and expensive upkeep would have ensured smaller successors had it not been for developments overseas. In 1870 the Russians laid down the first armoured cruiser, the *General Admiral*. She carried an armoured belt on the waterline but no protection for her four 8-inch and two 6-inch guns. The British answer to this theoretically very strong ship was the *Shannon*, a cruiser that was built to double as a battleship on foreign stations. In place of a waterline belt the *Shannon* had a protective deck: this arrangement became generally adopted in cruisers and was also used by the Americans in their dreadnought *Oklahoma*, laid down in 1912. The protective deck was a curved steel

deck; although only a few inches deep, its purpose was to deflect a hit upwards and away from vital machinery. Where the protective deck met the sides of the ship, it was below the waterline, but its apex above the line. For the next 20 years – the era of the protected cruiser – various classes were built and the classification of ships depended on the thickness of the protective deck.

Until the 1890s, there was a broad diversity in the size, gun power, armour and speed of protected cruisers. Some ships, such as the *Iris* and the *Mercury* – the first steel cruisers, laid down in 1878 – gave priority to speed. Making 18·6 knots, they were more than 4 knots faster than the battle fleet for which they were to scout. Within five years, however, cruisers of roughly the same displacement as these ships (3,730 tons) were demonstrating great fighting power as well as high speed. The Japanese *Takachiko*, built in Britain, carried two 10·3-inch and six 5·9-inch guns and had a 3-inch protective deck. She could make 18·5 knots and had a 9,000-mile range at 13 knots. Her displacement was only 3,650 tons.

At the end of the 1880s two developments led to increases in the size and cost of cruisers. Firstly, the introduction of Quick-Firing guns aided the process, for it meant that large, well-armed cruisers could not take on the older battleships

OPPOSITE ABOVE *The* Dupuy de Lôme *(1888), a French commerce raider capable, at 20 knots, of evading battleships and, with a 4-inch belt, of standing up to most cruisers.*
OPPOSITE, BELOW *HMS* Iris, *one of the first steel cruisers, laid down in 1878. Her 18·6-knot speed ensured that she was faster than the battle fleet she was designed to scout for.*
LEFT *HMS* Inconstant, *the first iron cruiser.*
BELOW *The French cruiser* Jeanne d'Arc, *built following the* Dupuy de Lôme's *success.*

carried without any loss of speed or other fighting qualities. Belt armour had the advantage that it tried to keep out shells rather than confine their damage once they had penetrated a ship. The armoured cruiser, as the next type was called, was largely an Anglo–Japanese enterprise. The Japanese were particularly interested in armoured cruisers for they were aware of the need to build up their fleet for the impending struggle with Russia, but lacked the finances to afford many battleships. Armoured cruisers, able to sustain even the heaviest hits, afforded a cheap means of acquiring powerful ships capable of taking on the older of the Russian battleships.

Britain's first armoured cruisers were specifically designed to counter the latest French ships, then from 1902 greater emphasis was given to offensive power. The *Monmouth* class carried 14 6-inch guns but the *Duke of*

with every hope of success. Secondly, there emerged the French *Guerre de course* school – firmly committed to the idea that raids on commercial shipping were the surest means of bringing Britain to her knees. This led the British to construct protector ships that were larger than the raiders produced by the French. To make their policy work the French, in 1888, ordered the *Dupuy de Lôme*. Displacing 6,300 tons, she carried two 7·6-inch and six 6·4-inch guns, all of which were carried in turrets with wide arcs of fire. Her 20 knots made her faster than contemporary battleships though a little slow compared to cruisers; but her 4-inch belt and turrets meant that she was much better protected. She was, in short, designed to stand up to cruisers and to evade battleships. This formidable ship was followed by the *Bruix* and the *Jeanne d'Arc*.

The British responded with a baffling variety of ships, the greatest of which were the *Powerful* and the *Terrible* and the *Diadem* class. The former two ships carried two 9·2-inch and 16 6-inch guns in the main armament and had 6 inches of deck armour. Their high speed of 22 knots made them extremely powerful commerce-protectors with a great range; but, being almost as big as the latest battleships, they were expensive to maintain. The *Diadems* were smaller and carried a uniform 6-inch armament.

These ships were the last of the protected cruisers, for the development of Krupp steel now enabled belt armour to be

Edinburgh, which displaced 12,600 tons, carried six 9·2-inch and 10 6-inch guns all of which were mounted singly. The *Warrior* class, laid down some two years later, carried six 9·2-inch and four powerful 7·5-inch guns which were carried on the upper deck where, unlike the 6-inch guns of the previous classes, they could be fought in any weather conditions. The subsequent *Minotaur* class carried four 9·2-inch and 10 7·5-inch guns.

The tasks of armoured cruisers in war were not particularly well defined, nor were they for their principal successors, the battlecruisers. Armoured cruisers were really too slow to be the fast supporting wing of the battle fleet and too slow to be good in a scouting role. Their replacement for most purposes by the battlecruiser did not entail the complete disappearance of cruisers. The battlecruiser was invaluable for certain tasks, but for reconnaissance another type was needed: this gap was filled by the light cruiser.

The first of the light cruisers was the German *Bremen*, which displaced 3,250 tons and carried 10 4·1-inch guns at a top speed of 23 knots. Subsequent improvements in speed led to the *Karlsruhe*, which was half as big again as the *Bremen* and made 29 knots. The British, on the other hand, placed greater store on defence and firepower. By the outbreak of war the British light cruiser had crept up to 5,400 tons and carried eight 6-inch guns.

WORLD WAR I

The Balance of Power at Sea, August 1914

By the time the nations went to war in 1914 several trends were discernible. The British had more ships than their enemies but they were not necessarily better ships. The various types of ship differed in both role and quality from nation to nation. In many respects, too, especially in the air and beneath the waves, all nations were unprepared for the war that was to follow. At its outbreak the strengths of the navies were as follows:

CATEGORY	BRITAIN	FRANCE	RUSSIA	JAPAN	ITALY	USA
Battleships	20	4	2	2	3	10
Battlecruisers	9	—	—	2	—	—
Pre-dreadnoughts	40	21	11	16	10	23
Heavy cruisers	47	19	8	12	5	21
Light cruisers	61	6	5	13	5	11
Destroyers	225	81	106	47	33	50
Submarines	75	67	36	18	14	39

CATEGORY	GERMANY	AUSTRIA–HUNGARY	TURKEY
Battleships	14	3	—
Battlecruisers	5	—	—
Pre-dreadnoughts	24	12	3
Heavy cruisers	27	3	—
Light cruisers	23	4	2
Destroyers	152	18	8
Submarines	30	11	—

HMS Nottingham *(1913), a Birmingham class light cruiser.*

ABOVE *HMS* Hogue *(1900), a Cressy
class cruiser seen in 1910; in September
1914 she was one of three British
cruisers sunk by the German U-boat
U-9.*
BELOW *The Japanese first-class
cruiser* Nisshin, *at Port Said in 1917.*

The War at Sea, 1914-1918

A Chronology

THE SYMBOL □ DENOTES ACTIVITY OVER A PERIOD OF TIME

1914

AUGUST

1   Germany declares war on Russia.

2   Germany declares war on France and invades Belgium.

4   Britain declares war on Germany.

4-9   Escape of German ships *Goeben* and *Breslau* to Constantinople.

12   Start of transportation of British Expeditionary Force to France.

15   First submarine sunk: *U-15* rammed by HMS *Birmingham*.

23   Japan declares war on Germany.

26   German signals book recovered by Russians from *Magdeburg*.

28   Battle of Heligoland Bight.

SEPTEMBER

□   ANZ forces occupy Samoa, New Guinea, Solomons and Bismarck Arch.

26   HM armoured cruisers *Cressy*, *Aboukir* and *Hogue* sunk by *U-9*.

OCTOBER

□   Japanese forces occupy Marshalls, Palau, Marianas and Carolines.

17   U-boat penetrates into Scapa Flow; Grand Fleet withdraws to Loch Swilly.

20   First merchant ship, the *Glitra*, sunk by U-boat (in this case by a boarding party from U-boat).

27   HMS *Audacious*, battleship, lost on a mine outside Loch Swilly.

28-9   Sortie by *Goeben* to attack Russian Black Sea ports.

NOVEMBER

1   Allied declaration of war on Turkey. Battle of Coronel.

2-6   Abortive British invasion at Tanga (East Africa).

3   First naval attack on Turkish forts at the Dardanelles; first German cruiser attack on English east coast.

6   British landings in Mesopotamia.

7   Capitulation of German fortress of Tsingtao to Japanese forces.

9   German cruiser *Emden* destroyed by *HMAS Sydney* after a two-month cruise during which she sank or captured 25 ships.

DECEMBER

8   Battle of Falkland Islands.

13   Turkish battleship *Messudieh* sunk by submarine *B-11*.

15   Abortive RN air attack on Cuxhaven base.

1915

JANUARY

25   Battle of Dogger Bank.

FEBRUARY

15   First naval assault at Dardanelles.

18   Opening of first submarine campaign against Allied commerce.

MARCH

18   Allied naval attack at Dardanelles flounders in minefield.

APRIL

□   Initiation of Otranto blockade by French Navy.

25   Landings on Gallipoli; Russian attacks on the Bosphorus.

MAY

7   Liner *Lusitania* sunk off Ireland by *U-20*.

23   Italy declares war on Austria-Hungary.

25   *U-21*, after entering Mediterranean from Germany, sinks HMS *Triumph* off Dardanelles.

JULY

10   German cruiser *Königsberg* sunk by monitors *Severn* and *Mersey* in Rufiji Delta, East Africa.

SEPTEMBER

1   First submarine campaign around British waters called off following sinking of the *Arabic*; U-boats concentrate in Mediterranean where few American ships are operating.

OCTOBER

16   Allied declaration of war on Bulgaria.

22   Withdrawal of German heavy units from the Baltic following sinking of *Prinz Adalbert* by British submarine *E-8*.

DECEMBER

1   Start of landings at Valona by Italians. Throughout the year there are continuous Russian attempts to sever the Zonguldak–Constantinople coal trade.

1916

JANUARY

□   Depth charges distributed to British warships.

8   Last sortie of the *Goeben* in the Black Sea.

9   Evacuation of the Dardanelles completed.

FEBRUARY

1   First British merchant ship lost to air attack.

21   Submarine offensive renewed.

MARCH

24   The *Sussex* sunk – an end to the submarine offensive.

APRIL-MAY

□   Laying of Dover mine barrage off Nieuport and the Scheldt in attempt to restrict passage of U-boats through Channel.

APRIL

18   Russian combined operation takes Trabzon, on Black Sea.

MAY-JUNE

31-1   Battle of Jutland.

JUNE

□   German surface reinforcements sent to the Channel.

AUGUST

19   Abortive sortie by German fleet in North Sea. Leads to withdrawal of fleet submarines to prepare for renewed commerce war.

OCTOBER

□   Renewed submarine offensive against commerce.

NOVEMBER

9-10   Seven German destroyers lost in single attack on Baltiski Port.

1917

JANUARY

□   Introduction of convoys on French coal-trade route (from south-coast ports of England to France) following 40% losses in December.

FEBRUARY

1   Germans launch unrestricted submarine warfare against commerce.

MARCH

12   Start of first Russian revolution. Provisional Government under Prince Lvov.

THE WAR AT SEA 1914-18

ALLIED POWERS (DATES DENOTE ENTRY INTO THE WAR)

CENTRAL POWERS

NEUTRAL POWERS

APRIL

6 USA declares war on Germany.

20 Last major German surface sortie in the Channel.

26 British Admiralty authorizes ocean-going convoys.

☐ Allies lose 430 ships (843,549 tons) during this month; merchant ship-to-submarine exchange-rate reaches 167:1.

MAY

4 First US destroyers arrive in Ireland.

10 First inward convoy from Gibraltar sails; regular Gibraltar convoys established in July.

24 First eastbound convoy leaves Hampton Road, Virginia.

AUGUST–JANUARY

☐ U-boat losses exceed replacement for first time (46:42).

AUGUST

☐ Outward convoys formed in attempt to combat heavy losses.

OCTOBER

12-17 German amphibious assault on Riga, the Russian's Baltic bridge head.

13 Peak of U-boat strength reached with 70 at sea.

NOVEMBER

☐ Convoys extended right into UK ports and not dispersed in Channel. Convoys introduced into Mediterranean. Arrival of US battle squadron at Scapa Flow.

7 Second Russian Revolution.

17 Last capital ship engagement between German and British forces.

21 Merchant ship losses reach lowest point since February.

DECEMBER

15 Russia and Germany agree armistice terms; Treaty of Brest–Litovsk takes Russia out of war in March 1918.

19 Start of deep mining and illumination of Dover barrage; German submarines forced to make 6-day passage around Scotland.

1918

JANUARY–NOVEMBER

☐ Shipbuilding exceeds losses by 1·75 m tons (4 m:2·25 m).

APRIL

1 Formation of RAF: Navy loses control of its air wing.

22-3 Zeebrugge raid.

23-4 Last sortie of German fleet.

MAY

☐ Exchange rate of merchantmen to submarines reaches lowest point (10:1).

JUNE

☐ Start of laying of North Sea barrage – 75% ready by November.

19 Austrian dreadnought *Szent Istvan* sunk by Italian *MB-21* off Pola.

SEPTEMBER

26 Bulgaria sues for armistice.

☐ Merchant shipping losses total 99.

OCTOBER

17-19 Belgian Army clears her coast of German naval bases.

27 Austria-Hungary sues for armistice.

29 Start of Kiel mutiny.

30 Armistice concluded with Turkey.

31 Revolution in Vienna and Budapest.

☐ Only 25 Allied merchantmen lost.

NOVEMBER

9 Revolution in Berlin.

10 Flight of Kaiser.

11 Armistice concluded with Germany.

21 Surrender of German fleet; internment of fleet in Scapa Flow.

1919

JANUARY

18 Assembly of Paris Peace Conference.

JUNE

21 German naval units scuttle themselves in Scapa Flow.

28 Germany signs Treaty of Versailles.

JULY

Blockade of Germany lifted.

Chapter Four

World War I

The war began at a time when the battleship had passed the peak of its powers. Some 10 years earlier armour and gunnery had been nearly absolute, the torpedo little more than a nuisance. During the Russo–Japanese War mines had accounted for many units whilst torpedoes had failed to live up to expectations. But subsequent improvements, combined with the proven power of mines, prompted the British to revise their traditional policy of closely blockading an enemy coast. In the summer of 1914 an interim policy of observational blockade across the lower part of the North Sea was discarded in favour of a more distant blockade of Germany based on Scapa Flow and Dover. It was clear evidence of the fear instilled by underwater weapons that such changes had to be made.

At sea the Great War was largely deadlocked: British guns and German underwater weapons cancelled each other out with little apparent advantage to either side. Britain's overwhelming superiority in surface ships was to some extent neutralized by the Germans' refusal to risk

BELOW *The sinking of HMS* Audacious, *lost on a mine outside Loch Swilly on 27 October 1914.*
OPPOSITE *Two German torpedo successes. In the upper picture the flotilla leader HMS* Scott, *a destroyer, is hit by a German submarine in the North Sea, 15 August 1918. In the lower picture an Allied steamship is struck by a torpedo from the German submarine* U-35.

battle and by their defensive minefields laid in the southern North Sea. Until Germany's heavy ships were eliminated, British light forces could not penetrate deep into Heligoland Bight to clear the minefields and lay new ones that would confine German units to their harbours; nor could major surface units be moved to other theatres as long as the German Navy remained intact. The Germans were prepared to risk action but only after mines and torpedoes had taken such a toll of British ships that such actions had a reasonable chance of success; in fact this never happened. Instead the Germans adopted a more passive policy, allowing the presence of their fleet to tie down its British counterpart while the active prosecution of the war was left in the hands of the submariners.

Britain's greatest single advantage over Germany and Austria-Hungary during World War I lay in her geographical position. By holding Dover, Scapa Flow, Gibraltar and Suez, she effectively controlled German and Austrian communications with the outside world. From 4 August 1914 Britain imposed an economic blockade of the Central Powers that increased in severity with each year of the war and was a major factor in bringing about victory. It was not, however, fully effective until the entry, in 1917, of the USA into the war – an event which enabled the Allies completely to disregard the rights of neutrals. Up to that time Britain had had to be careful not to offend neutrals, particularly the USA, and this had allowed some loopholes

in the blockade. To close them the British had tried to restrict neutral trade with Germany and even to buy cargoes outright in order to stop them finishing up in enemy hands. Such actions had been of dubious legality and had caused offence; but on every occasion when difficulties arose with the Americans, the Germans had turned opinion against themselves by their practice of conducting restricted submarine campaigns against commercial shipping moving into Britain. The campaigns were introduced as a retaliatory measure against the British blockade of Germany. Because of them neutral nations, including America, suffered losses for which, not unnaturally, Germany was blamed; the best-known single incident was probably the sinking of the *Lusitania*, in which 128 American citizens lost their lives.

The initial successes of the U-boats, despite the restrictions placed on them, led to mounting pressure in Germany in support of an *un*restricted campaign, which after the bloodily indecisive battles before Verdun and on the Somme, seemed to offer Germany her best hope of victory. At the time the German Naval Staff estimated that, unrestricted, the U-boats could sink 600,000 tons of shipping every month. This was a rate of loss far beyond the Allies' replacement capacity and would be sufficient to scare off neutral trade with Britain. Even if the USA entered the war, the Germans believed that the campaign would bring Britain to her knees before American help could become effective.

During the earlier restricted campaigns Allied countermeasures proved of little use. Until 1916 there was no means of detecting a submerged submarine; nor was there a satisfactory anti-submarine weapon. The Allies ceaselessly patrolled the sea lanes in anticipation of action but the submarines easily evaded the patrols and waited for the single, unescorted merchantmen that were certain to sail past

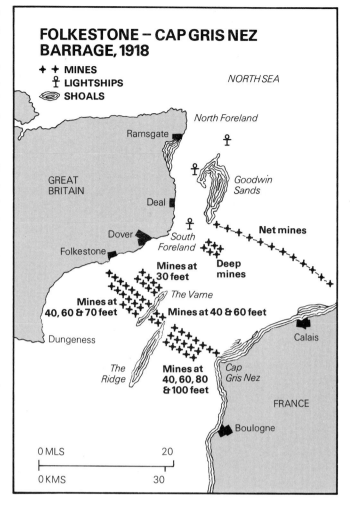

FOLKESTONE – CAP GRIS NEZ BARRAGE, 1918
✚ ✚ MINES
⚓ LIGHTSHIPS
🜲 SHOALS

ABOVE *The map shows how the Allies used mines to deny the German fleet access to the Channel; to the north there was a blockade based on Scapa Flow.*
BELOW *German U-boats in Kiel Harbour in October 1918; later that month the German fleet mutinied.*

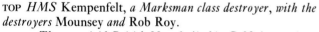

TOP *HMS* Kempenfelt, *a Marksman class destroyer, with the destroyers* Mounsey *and* Rob Roy.
ABOVE *The non-rigid British Naval Airship C-23A escorting an outward-bound convoy off the coast of Cornwall in December 1917. The convoy system, introduced in June that year, brought a dramatic cut in losses to U-boats and helped to save Britain from the spectre of starvation.*

sooner or later. Only a defensively armed merchant ship stood much chance of escaping the submarines: successful evasions sometimes occurred because submarines preferred to try and stop ships and sink them by gunfire or explosives rather than deplete their limited number of torpedoes.

Three factors helped to contain the number of U-boat sinkings during the restricted campaigns. These were, firstly, the limited number of U-boats at sea; secondly, the limited nature of their armament and endurance, and, thirdly, political considerations.

Once the political restrictions were lifted, the German submarines were able to sink nearly 2,000,000 tons of ship-

ping in the three months after 1 February 1917. British counter-measures continued to have little success until the introduction of convoys – a decision taken in April as a result of political pressure on the Admiralty. After disastrous losses on the cross-Channel coal trade in the last months of 1916, the French insisted that the British adopt a convoy system on that route. Convoys were started and losses fell drastically in the first quarter of 1917. Encouraged, the British became more positive: they saw how few ocean-going ships left the United Kingdom each week (about 130) and realized how relatively easy it would be to provide escorts for them. The convoy system was soon applied to both inward and outward sailings and gradually, through its extension, the submarine menace was controlled – even though it was never beaten. Other contributory factors were Britain's severe food rationing programme, her strict allocation of cargo spaces and her ruthless concentration of shipping on the North Atlantic route. Losses were thereby reduced to a level that could be covered by American ship construction.

During the war the Germans sank 12,850,814 tons of shipping, of which 7,750,000 tons were British; but despite this huge total they failed to sink sufficient numbers of ships escorted in convoys. Of the 16,070 ships that sailed in ocean convoys only 96 were lost, and only 161 out of the 67,888 ships that sailed in coastal convoys. Losses among stragglers and ships sailing independently were heavier but not enough to give Germany victory. On the other hand submarine losses were fairly severe: nearly half the submarines commissioned during the war – 178 out of 373 – were sunk, though only for a short time did their losses exceed their rate of replacement. The reason why the unrestricted campaign failed was not because of the losses taken by the U-boats, but because they failed to maintain the rate of

49

sinkings that was achieved for a brief period between February and April 1917.

Improvements in design and the discovery of new techniques were naturally accelerated by the war. Some developments were quite strange. There was a seaplane carrier with auxiliary sails; and torpedo craft equipped with spiked tracks so that they could scale nets and booms. Submarines were built with 12-inch guns that could be fired when awash and there were fleet submarines whose steam engines gave a surface speed of 25 knots but which took 30 minutes to dive. Other exotic ideas included experiments with pink camouflage paint and patrol craft with similar stems and sterns.

But the oddities were outnumbered by more serious and important developments. The war encouraged numerous increases in the size of ships and also specialized designs. By 1916 the British had plans for a 36,000-ton battlecruiser and had built ships with 18-inch guns. The *Renown* class battlecruiser reached 30 knots and destroyers were approaching 40 knots. Submarines grew in size so that by the summer of 1916 they could operate out of Germany as far as the east coast of the United States. Mine-laying submarines made their début in 1915, and purpose-built minesweepers and minelayers increased in numbers and importance. Monitors and armed merchant cruisers proliferated, as did patrol-boats and Q-ships (armed merchantmen used as submarine decoys), but the most important developments for the future took place in the air and beneath the surface of the sea.

As early as 1915 the British developed two counters to the submarine: one was a means of destruction and the other a method of detection. A passive listening device, called the hydrophone, provided the first means of detecting a sub-

Naval aircraft and the evolution of the carrier.
ABOVE *Lieutenant C. R. Samson makes the first take-off from the deck of a British warship (HMS* Africa*) in January 1912.*
OPPOSITE, ABOVE *A Short Folder seaplane being lifted out of the hold of HMS* Ark Royal.
BELOW AND OPPOSITE, BELOW *An aerial view of the aircraft carrier HMS* Furious *and the scene as a Sopwith Pup lands on the after flight deck. Note the Pup's skid undercarriage and the vertical arrester wires fixed to the deck.*

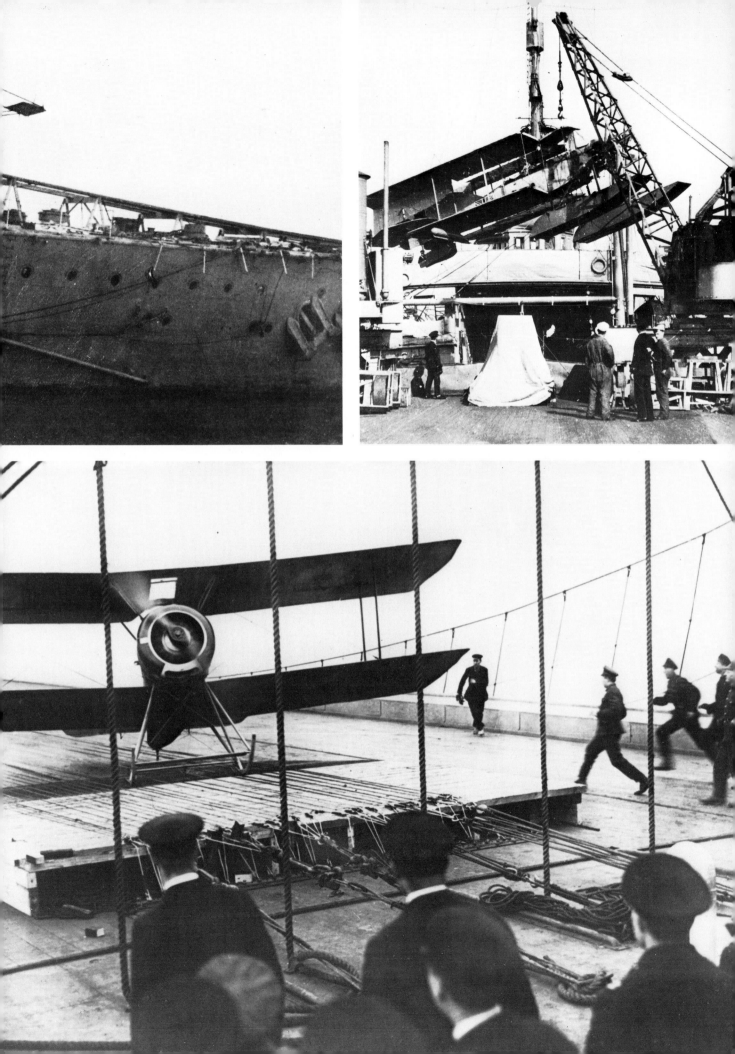

ABOVE *Accident on the high seas – HMS* Campania *sinks after being rammed by HMS* Glorious, *5 May 1918.*

merged submarine. But its value was limited because the ship carrying the hydrophone had to be stopped before it could pick up the sound of the submarine's propellers, and several ships were needed to work together before an accurate position could be calculated. Unfortunately, no other method of detection was available during the war, although in mid-1917 the British carried out trials with an active search device known as Asdic; this, however, did not come into service before the end of the war.

The depth-charge brought the first really effective method of destroying a submerged U-boat other than by ramming. It consisted of a heavy high-explosive charge designed to go off at a depth of between 40 and 80 feet by means of a hydrostatically controlled detonator. It entered service in January 1916 and it made its first kill on 26 March when *U-68* was sunk by the Q-ship *Farnborough*. On 6 July *UC-7* gained the dubious distinction of being the first victim of a successful combination of hydrophones and depth-charges. These methods of detection and destruction became increasingly effective after the introduction of convoys. In their hunt for merchantmen, submarines could no longer rely on picking off helpless independent ships but had to attack the escorted ships – a process that naturally exposed them to counter-attack from the new weapons.

Perhaps the most remarkable fact about the convoy system was that, of the ships lost, only five were sunk when

aircraft were present – despite the latter's very limited offensive power. During the war aircraft registered many 'firsts'. Japanese seaplanes achieved the first sinking of a warship from air attack when a small German minelayer was sunk at Tsingtao in 1914; and seaplanes from the *Ark Royal* spotted for naval gunfire at the Dardanelles for the first time on 1 March 1915. On 12 August aerial torpedoes claimed their

BELOW *HMS* Furious, *after conversion, steams through heavy seas; her outline is now more recognizably that of a modern carrier.*

first victim – a grounded ship – and three days later, again at the Dardanelles, sank ships with sea room. In the Baltic, the Germans carried out the first successful bombing of a battleship on 27 April 1916 – a Russian pre-dreadnought being heavily damaged. In the spring of 1917 both the Russians and Germans started aerial mining.

The successful use of aircraft prompted two developments – the search for a vessel capable of operating aircraft and the mounting of anti-aircraft guns in heavy ships. Although France was the first nation to commission a (seaplane) carrier, with the *Le Foudre* in 1913, it was the Royal Navy that quickly seized the lead in this field and carried out much of the early experimentation. The planes did not fly off the deck of the first British seaplane carrier, the *Ark Royal* – a converted collier – but were winched out of the ship onto the sea, where they took off. The system then operated in reverse when the aircraft returned from its mission. This clumsy and long-winded process proved a major deficiency with the slow-moving *Ark Royal*, since she could not load and unload seaplanes and at the same time keep up with the fleet and so carry out her reconnaissance role. Fast cross-Channel steamers were converted to carriers on the outbreak of war, but it was from an ex-Cunarder, the *Campania*, that the next major breakthrough occurred, when in August 1915 an aircraft with wheeled floats took off from her forward deck.

The true function of the seaplane and the carrier was reconnaissance. By 1917 the task of air defence had been handed over to aircraft that were carried on the cruisers and capital ships of the Grand Fleet. These aircraft were wheeled and had a considerably superior performance to the seaplane, but, unlike the latter, they could not be recovered. The concept of an aircraft taking off from and landing on a flight-deck took a long time to be accepted. The first experiment in deck landing was carried out on 2 August 1917. An attempt to repeat the performance three days later cost the pilot his life. In order to try to avoid such accidents, the British built two different types of flight-decks into ships. To the *Furious*, on whose fore-deck the previous experiments had taken place, a separate landing-deck was added behind the funnel. This proved unsatisfactory because the turbulence from the funnels made landings unreasonably hazardous. Next the *Argus*, then under construction, was given a continuous free deck clear of any obstruction, but unfortunately the ship was completed too late to see action. For the duration of World War I landings on the surface of the sea, from where the planes were winched aboard, remained the only means of recovery.

Nevertheless, with the *Argus* the British had evolved the prototype aircraft carrier. There were still major problems to overcome but the basic concept had been settled. After the war the fitting of catapults (which had begun in 1912 in the US Navy), the evolution of arrester gear and the location of bridge and funnels were problems that were met and overcome by the navies of the Great Powers. That of the location of bridge and funnels was possibly the most serious, and various attempts were made to clear smoke and fumes away from the flight-deck through side vents. It was not until the British developed the island structure, offset to starboard, that the matter could be resolved. This arrangement was generally followed in other navies though the Japanese did build carriers with port-side islands.

The first carrier with an island structure was the *Eagle*, which entered service in the Royal Navy in 1923. Soon, however, the Royal Navy went into a period of relative decline. It had lost control over its air arm in 1918 and a series of stringent post-war budgets deprived it of money for research and development in the field of aviation. In the meantime other navies were more favoured. In December 1922 the Japanese completed the first purpose-built carrier, the *Hosho*. The implications were clear; and, indeed, from about that time the Japanese and American navies overtook Britain and left her behind in the development of aircraft carriers.

Surface Actions

Throughout the war, and in every theatre, there were regular clashes between the light forces of the various navies. Throughout the war, too, all combatants tried to use their submarines to reduce the forces opposed to them, though in no theatre did the latter policy enjoy lasting success.

Little, in fact, happened in the course of the war at sea to alter the fundamental *status quo*. The supremacy of the British Grand Fleet was rarely disturbed even by its chief opponent, the German High Seas Fleet, which remained largely bottled up in its home waters for the duration of the war. Indeed, so daunting was the destructive power of the heavy ships on either side that in no theatre was an inferior fleet prepared consistently to challenge a superior one. Nor were the superior navies ever in a position to compel the enemy to come out and give battle.

Even when navies did meet on the open sea, the theoretical likelihood of a battle being decisive was small: given that one of the parties was inferior and would therefore wish to break off contact quickly, there was little the other could do – lacking the present-day indispensables of radar, a good communications system and adequate night-fighting equipment – to press home its advantage. Only in the Anglo–German struggle did any major conflicts occur – and for the most part these were not willingly sought by the Germans.

BELOW *Survivors take to the water and pack the side of the doomed German cruiser* Blücher, *which sank at the Battle of Dogger Bank, 25 January 1915.*
OPPOSITE *At the Battle of the Falkland Islands, on 8 December 1914, HMS* Inflexible *stands by while survivors from the German cruiser* Gneisenau *are rescued from the icy waters; 190 men out of the ship's complement of 764 were saved. This photograph was taken from the battlecruiser HMS* Invincible, *which also took part in the rescue operation.*

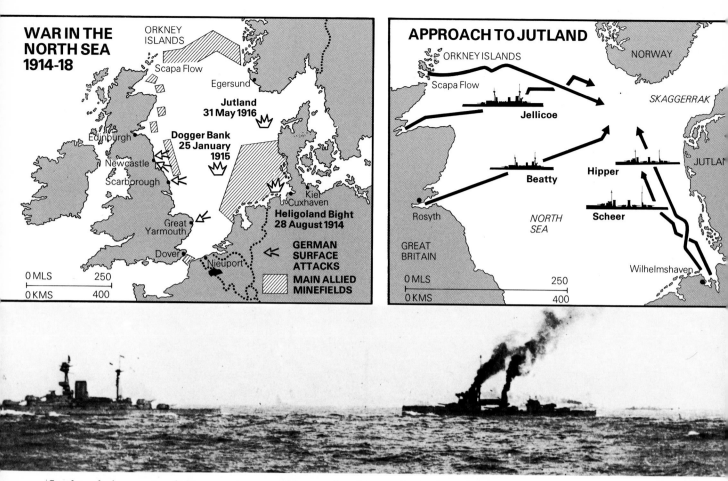

WAR IN THE NORTH SEA 1914-18

ORKNEY ISLANDS
Scapa Flow
Egersund
Jutland 31 May 1916
Dogger Bank 25 January 1915
Edinburgh
Newcastle
Scarbrough
Great Yarmouth
Dover
Nieuport
Kiel
Cuxhaven
Heligoland Bight 28 August 1914
GERMAN SURFACE ATTACKS
MAIN ALLIED MINEFIELDS

0 MLS 250
0 KMS 400

APPROACH TO JUTLAND

ORKNEY ISLANDS
NORWAY
Scapa Flow
SKAGGERRAK
Jellicoe
Beatty
Hipper
JUTLAN
Scheer
Rosyth
NORTH SEA
GREAT BRITAIN
Wilhelmshaven

0 MLS 250
0 KMS 400

In the whole course of the war, no more than two battles were fought to the bitter end, and both of these happened in non-European waters.

The first battle of the war was a dashing action fought in August 1914 by British battlecruisers and light forces against German light forces engaged in mine warfare in the Heligoland Bight. It was a confused battle fought among shifting fog banks, a battle noted for its astonishingly bad staff work, and one which had little material effect but a profound influence on morale. In numerical terms the British sank three light cruisers – the *Köln*, *Mainz* and *Ariadne* – and one destroyer at no cost to their own fleet. More important, however, was the fact that the battle, fought on Germany's doorstep, confirmed the Royal Navy in its sense of ascendancy over the German fleet. Fortunately for the Royal Navy, its confidence was not unduly shaken in the following month when three of its armoured cruisers – the *Aboukir*, *Cressy* and *Hogue* – were lost to a single submarine, the *U-9*.

The two decisive actions mentioned above were fought in November and December 1914 off the coasts of South America. In the first, Admiral von Spee's German cruiser squadron, fleeing from superior forces in the Far East, met and annihilated an inferior force of hastily commissioned British cruisers at the Battle of Coronel off the coast of Chile, the British losing two armoured cruisers and one armed merchant cruiser.

In the following month the German squadron was caught, in its turn, by a superior British force that had been assembled and dispatched at great speed to the South Atlantic by the British Admiralty. It included two battlecruisers, the *Inflexible* and *Invincible*, which were supported by two armoured and two light cruisers and one armed merchant cruiser. Von Spee was caught off the Falkland Islands and the *Scharnhorst* and *Gneisenau* were sunk, together with two light cruisers, the *Nürnberg* and *Leipzig*. Another light cruiser, the *Dresden*, escaped but was later caught and scuttled by her crew to avoid capture.

On 24 January 1915 the first conflict between heavy units in European waters took place at the Battle of Dogger Bank. The Germans, attempting an attack on Britain's east coast (their third in the war) were intercepted by a superior British force of five battlecruisers. During the action the Germans lost an armoured cruiser, the *Blücher*, but three battlecruisers escaped, mainly because of the poor signalling of the British flagship. In the euphoria of victory this point was largely ignored, as was, in British circles at least, the need for anti-flash protection to guard the magazines from exploding after a hit. The Germans, on the other hand, saw the value of such protection, with the result that the balance of losses was reversed in the next engagement.

This action was the Battle of Jutland. Although on the day it proved something of a non-event, Jutland stands as a crucial encounter in that, on 31 May 1916, for the first and

The Battle of Jutland, 31 May–1 June 1916

At Jutland – the only time the main battle fleets fought each other in the entire war – the British hoped to use their naval might to score a crushing victory. Such were the risks, however, that Admiral Jellicoe, the British commander, was, as Churchill put it, 'the only man on either side who could lose the war in an afternoon'. But, as the tables show, Jellicoe would have had to have lost calamitously for the balance of naval power to be reversed. In reality Jellicoe was cautious and the losses, though heavy, were roughly proportionate to those suffered in the other principal surface actions of the war.

1 THE BALANCE OF FORCES			2 LOSSES	
CATEGORY	BRITISH GRAND FLEET	GERMAN HIGH SEAS FLEET	BRITISH	GERMAN
Battleships	28	16	—	—
Battlecruisers	9	5	3	1
Pre-dreadnoughts	—	6	—	1
Armoured cruisers	8	—	3	—
Light cruisers	26	11	—	4
Destroyers	78	61	8	4
Seaplane carriers	1	—	—	—
Totals	150	99	14	10

OPPOSITE *The British battleships* Royal Oak *and* Hercules *at Jutland, their guns trained to starboard. A notable difference between the two is that one is making smoke and is coal-powered while the other, being oil-powered, has a clear funnel.*
BELOW *The battlecruiser HMS* Indefatigable *going into the Battle of Jutland.*

only time in the war, the world's major contending navies came, if briefly, in range of each other.

The battle came about as a result of wireless interceptions made by the British, the history of which goes back to the sinking of the *Magdeburg* in August 1914 and the acquisition by the British of the German ship's code-books, which gave them more than a headstart in subsequent intelligence work. However, nearly two years later, contact on a telling scale with the German High Seas Fleet still eluded the British. Then wireless messages were received which suggested that a major German fleet movement was in progress. The Grand Fleet put to sea and on the next day Admiral Beatty's advance screen of battlecruisers came up against the decoy battlecruisers of Admiral Hipper. The Germans in fact planned to lure part of the main British fleet to oppose Hipper and then to strike with the superior weight of the High Seas Fleet, which for the present was tailing Hipper some 50 miles to the south.

The battlecruisers fought an initial action and the British lost heavily: the magazines of the *Indefatigable* and *Queen Mary* exploded, and the *Lion* was narrowly saved from a similar end, her magazines being flooded just in time. After having made contact with Admiral Scheer's main fleet, Beatty led the enemy northwards with the result that there followed two brief engagements between the main fleets, in which the Germans suffered a severe battering but managed to escape under cover of night and regain their ports in safety.

The battle was a great disappointment to the British, whose superiority in numbers, gun power and tactics had seemed likely to bring success; but failures in communication, and a general inability to appreciate the enemy's intentions, combined to deny Britain a decisive victory. Although their losses were greater than the Germans', the British retained a secure command over the surface of the world's oceans; thereafter the Germans confined their efforts to a few sorties of little significance until the surrender of November 1918.

Chapter Five
The Inter-War Years

By the end of World War I the bonds that had linked Britain, Japan and the United States were being loosened. The defeat of Germany and the destruction of her Navy in Scapa Flow did not lead to a general reduction of naval strengths. Instead, conflicting ambitions grew more and more apparent and, in the resulting atmosphere of suspicion and distrust, erstwhile allies began to look at each other as future enemies.

Although Britain was impoverished by the war, Japan and the United States emerged from it with greatly increased industrial power. Both, moreover, nurtured interests and ambitions in the western Pacific which the war had done nothing to reconcile; and by 1918 both nations had embarked on warship construction programmes whose products seemed destined to be used against each other at some unspecified date.

Earlier, in 1915, the Japanese had announced their '8–8' programme of 16 battleships and battlecruisers. These ships were to have a life expectancy of only eight years; in other words, they were scheduled to expire long before they were worn out. But if the Japanese then chose to build new ships at the end of the eight-year period without scrapping those already in existence, they could, within a decade, build a fleet so strong that it would completely dominate the Far East.

The USA, on the other hand, was determined to have a navy 'second to none', and to achieve this she had, in August 1916, ordered 10 battleships. Although only three had been laid down by the end of 1919, these at least kept pace with the Japanese in terms of armament: each now had the 16-inch gun.

Britain, meanwhile, sought equality with the other leading naval powers but was really in no position to maintain parity. Although after the war she had a numerical superiority, it was founded on 11 old capital ships, armed with 12-inch guns, that were in fact worn out, obsolete and in need of immediate replacement if she was to retain her relative position. Given her impoverished state, Britain could ill afford a massive building programme. However, developments in the Pacific forced her hand. In 1921 she

Inter-war treaties limited both the numbers and size of warships, and those nations that kept within the limits had to renovate their older ships and devise fresh concepts for their new ones. Thus, in an effort to save weight, British ships like the Rodney (below), carried all their main armament forward in triple turrets, while the Warspite (right), emerged in 1937 totally transformed from her 1915 appearance.

ABOVE *The Japanese battleship* Kongo.

ABOVE RIGHT *HMS* Nelson; *like the Rodney (previous page) her main armament was carried forward in triple turrets.*

RIGHT *The US battleship* Washington, *an inter-war design which incorporated nine 16-inch guns.*

BELOW *The battlecruiser HMS* Hood *on trials.*

BELOW RIGHT *The* Dunkerque, *a French battleship of the inter-war period, armed with 13-inch guns and capable of making 30 knots; when the Germans occupied France in World War II she was broken up to provide steel for Germany.*

OPPOSITE, BOTTOM RIGHT *The German battleship* Bismarck, *laid down in 1936, puts to sea in 1941 on what was to be her last voyage.*

laid down four 48,000-ton battlecruisers and programmed battleships with 18-inch guns – a move designed to counter Japan's proposed *Class 13* battlecruisers that were to have a 13-inch armour belt, 30 knots and eight 18-inch guns.

By 1921 the capital ships being built and projected would have cost the Great Powers over £250 million, and costs were rising. The USA, anxious to avoid a heavy programme of construction, found herself in the fortunate (if paradoxical) position of being able, through her ability to outbuild her rivals if the need arose, to force the other nations into agreeing to limit their armaments. The British were willing enough to limit theirs, but the Japanese were less keen. Not only were the Japanese programmes nearer completion than those of the other nations, their statesmen also disliked the limit proposed for their navy and suspected, quite correctly, that there were racialist undercurrents in the common Anglo–American policy.

However, despite Japanese reservations, the Washington Treaty of 1921 fixed a balance between the fleets of the world and placed limits on the sizes of ships. With certain exceptions no capital ships were then laid down before 1931, by which time the Depression had emptied the world's treasuries and so delayed any new construction for a while. At the 1930 London Conference, new building was put back until after January 1937 – although France and Italy were each allowed two new ships. The Great Powers, meanwhile, were confined to refitting and rebuilding their existing ships.

The rebuilding programmes of the various navies followed roughly similar lines. Increasing concern about aerial and torpedo attack dictated a thickening of deck armour, increased bulges, augmented anti-aircraft defences and the fitting of aircraft and hangars into capital ships. The Japanese, with a smaller number of ships, rebuilt more extensively than did the Western navies. The *Nagato* was the most powerful ship in the world when she was completed in 1920. She was refitted in 1924 and rebuilt between 1934 and 1936. During the refit her distinctive pagoda

bridge was given more platforms and her forward funnel was trunked; in the rebuilding phase, triple bottoms and increased bulges added to her passive defence whilst deck armour was doubled and turret protection increased by 50 per cent. The pagoda was extensively rebuilt and enlarged and the anti-aircraft armament was increased. The range of elevation of her 16-inch guns was raised to 43°. Tonnage increased by 6,300 tons but speed did not fall away because she was re-boilered and re-engined and changed over to oil. The rebuilding of all the big Japanese ships conformed to this basic pattern.

With the exception of the *California* and *Maryland* classes, the American ships were all rebuilt. Most of them lost their distinctive cage masts: in their place tripod superstructures were built up, and anti-aircraft defences were increased and the ships re-engined to burn oil. The British were less thorough. Many of the fast *Queen Elizabeth* class were ultimately rebuilt, but none of the *Revenge* ships was substantially altered[1]. Those British ships that were rebuilt failed to hold their speed as the American and Japanese ships had done; although their armour was thickened, little could disguise their all-round inferiority to their contemporaries. At the time the

battlecruiser *Hood* was Britain's, and the world's, greatest warship; but despite this, and perhaps because of it, no major refit was completed before World War II. Her side armour was by then obsolete, and her deck armour was anyway minimal. Her graceful lines and fine profile did not make up for her lack of protection.

Italian and French ships contained several novel features. They were, by Pacific standards, under-protected. But whereas the Italian *Vittorio Veneto* was very well armed with nine (3 × 3) 15-inch guns, the French *Dunkerque* and *Strasbourg* carried only 13-inch guns. There were eight of these, and they were all carried forward of the bridge, in the same manner as the *Nelson* class. The French ships could make 30 knots but the graceful, lightweight *Vittorio Veneto* could reach 35 knots.

The ending, in 1937, of the limitations on capital ship building led the nations once more to go their separate ways. The British, pressed by the deteriorating European situation, adopted the 14-inch gun for their new 33,000-ton battleships, which were laid down in 1937. Initially they were to carry 12 guns in three turrets, two forward and one aft, but the need for increased armour caused the superimposed forward turret to be reduced to a twin. In 1936 the Germans – who formerly had observed the limitations of the Versailles Treaty – laid down the *Bismarck* and *Tirpitz*. These ships followed the gun

[1] In fact by 3 September 1939 only *Warspite* had been rebuilt; *Barham* was barely altered; *Malaya* had a hangar added; the *Valiant* was commissioned in October 1939, and the *Queen Elizabeth* in July 1940.

arrangement of the last German class to be laid down some 20 years before – eight 15-inch guns in four twin turrets. The Americans, on the other hand, combined the 16-inch gun with the triple turret; the new *Washington* class carried nine 16-inch guns. These very impressive ships displaced 35,000 tons[1], carried 20 5-inch dual-purpose (DP) guns[2] and an 18-inch armour belt.

But even the Americans were dwarfed by Japan's new ships. Depending on quality to offset their inferiority in numbers, the Japanese built the *Yamato* and *Musashi*. Both ships were completed after the raid on Pearl Harbor (December 1941). They displaced 64,000 tons, made 27 knots and carried nine (3 × 3) 18·1-inch guns that could fire a 3,200-pound shell nearly 25 miles. The main belt was over 16 inches thick and turret-face armour exceeded 25 inches. Deck protection was up to 9 inches. Only 53 per

[1] The 35,000-ton figure is the one given in the US Navy lists, but it seems that this is a deliberate understatement. It is hard to see how ships with these characteristics could displace so little when other nations were exceeding 35,000 tons for ships of lesser power.
[2] Dual-purpose guns could be used in two capacities – anti-ship and anti-aircraft.

LEFT *A view of the German cruiser* Leipzig *on her way to make a courtesy visit to Portsmouth in 1934; she was designed as a powerful commerce raider and carried a main armament of 5·9-inch guns (this was within the limitations that had been imposed on German shipbuilding by the Treaty of Versailles).*
ABOVE *Aircraft trials being carried out from HMS* Illustrious; *although better protected than the carriers of other nations, the* Illustrious *was handicapped by her low aircraft capacity – she could carry only 36 planes on a displacement of 23,000 tons.*
OPPOSITE, ABOVE *HMS* Argonaut, *a Dido class cruiser equipped with high-angle guns.*
OPPOSITE, BELOW *Two carrier profiles. The upper picture shows HMS* Illustrious, *and the lower picture features the Japanese carrier* Shokaku, *with her heavy anti-aircraft defences.*

cent of the waterline was covered by the belt but protection was augmented by having 1,147 watertight compartments. These two battleships, the only ones to be completed out of a class of four, were intended to be the last word in battleship design, exceeding as they would any American ship capable of using the Panama Canal. Unfortunately for the Japanese, by the time they were built they were obsolescent; the balance of power had shifted to the carrier and its aircraft.

Until 1939 the Royal Navy retained a numerical superiority in aircraft carriers over any other navy. This failed to disguise, however, the obsolescence of her carrier aircraft and their small numbers as compared to the American and Japanese navies. And although the carriers themselves were numerous, they were small in carrying capacity. HMS *Eagle* (22,600 tons) carried a maximum of 21 aircraft, and the *Courageous*, despite having been programmed for 52 aircraft, could handle only 33. Such figures seem especially low beside their Japanese and American counterparts. The *Kaga* may be taken as representative of Japanese carriers: she, like many of the earlier carriers, was a converted capital ship; she displaced

27,000 tons and carried 60 aircraft. A refit between 1934 and 1935 added another 11,000 tons and space for 30 more aircraft. Meanwhile the Americans had the *Lexington* (36,000 tons), which carried 72 aircraft – and later was able to carry 90.

When building restarted in the mid-1930s, the same pattern was repeated. Although the 22,000-ton British carrier *Ark Royal* could handle 60 aircraft, the Japanese *Hiryu* (only 16,000 tons), could carry 13 more and the USS *Enterprise* (20,000 tons) operated 80. Unfortunately for the British, further ground was lost with their next carriers, the *Illustrious* class. The first of this class carried only 36 aircraft on 23,000 tons. On the other hand, British carriers were more heavily armoured than those of other nations. American carriers were protected only along the waterline and over machinery spaces; the *Illustrious* had heavy flight-deck protection (3 inches) and the magazines and hangars were protected by 4·5 inches of armour. However, in view of the weakness of Britain's carrier aircraft, the carriers needed this protection.

Until the entry of the monoplane into service, Britain's inferiority in the air was not too marked either in terms of quality or quantity; but Japan and the USA had meanwhile pressed ahead in the theory and practice of carrier operations. The two Pacific powers were conscious that aircraft would be very important in the future and might play an independent role in the next war; whereas the British saw the aircraft as a support for the battleship and

BELOW *The sleek lines of the Italian cruiser* Zara; *like many Italian warships, she was built for speed and could make 34 knots.*

RIGHT *The German commerce raider* Deutschland; *laid down in 1929, she was the first of a new type referred to as 'pocket battleships'; her main armament consisted of six 11-inch guns. She is seen here at Gibraltar in 1937.*

OPPOSITE, FAR RIGHT *The German cruiser* Köln; *her main armament was similar to that of the* Leipzig *(see previous page).*

OPPOSITE, BELOW *By 1936, when this photograph was taken, Germany was under Nazi rule, and elaborate ceremonies were held to mark the launching of major additions to the Führer's fleet. The picture shows the* Scharnhorst *at Wilhelmshaven.*

not as a possible threat to its superiority. Furthermore, the Japanese and Americans were conscious of the need for specialized aircraft, and recognized the need for dive-bombers, torpedo-bombers and fighters. The British tried to make their aircraft double up on duties, with the result that their performance was substantially inferior to those of the other powers.

From 1936 onwards the Royal Navy's difficulties increased: while other navies were equipped with mono-planes her own partner, the Royal Air Force, took most of Britain's modern aircraft. In 1939 the Royal Navy had only one type of monoplane in service. This was the Skua, a multi-role aircraft unable to discharge any single task well. The recce aircraft was the Osprey, a two-seater biplane introduced in 1932. Land-based aircraft were similarly inferior to contemporaries and the shortage of aircraft was crippling. In 1939 the Royal Navy had 300 aircraft; by comparison, in 1941 – when they went to war – the Americans had over 5,000 and the Japanese over 3,200.

Perhaps it was inevitable that once the Washington Treaty had limited their battlefleets the nations should attempt to outbuild one another in cruisers, which, though limited by the Treaty in terms of displacement (10,000 tons) and gun power (8-inch guns), were not for the time being limited in numbers built.

The Japanese and Americans both built up to and beyond Treaty limitations. The former began with the Kako class, laid down in 1922. These ships mounted 7·9-inch guns in single turrets (these were doubled in a refit in 1939). Then, with the *Ashigara* class, the Japanese exceeded Treaty limits from the outset. The four ships of this class displaced 10,900 tons (after a 1940 refit over 13,000 tons) and carried 10 7·9-inch and six 4·7-inch guns. Twelve torpedo tubes and two aircraft completed an impressive offensive capability. The ships could make over 35 knots and had up to 5 inches of deck armour and a 4-inch belt.

The Americans built roughly similar craft. In the *Pensacola* class 10 8-inch guns were fitted in twin and triple turrets; later the *Northampton* class carried weight-saving triple turrets which gave these 9,000-ton cruisers nine 8-inch guns. When the Japanese moved to smaller guns for their cruisers the Americans immediately followed. The *Mogami*, laid down in 1931, carried 15 (5 × 3) 6·1-inch and eight 5-inch DP guns; but this proved to be to the detriment of stability and she was subsequently given a main armament of 10 8-inch guns. The *Brooklyn* carried the same number of 6-inch weapons. However, the Americans did not follow the *Tone* class. These unique Japanese cruisers carried all their armament forward and operated five aircraft from a clear flying-off deck aft.

The British, on the other hand, were reluctant to build cruisers with 8-inch guns simply because that was the maximum size that could be laid down. However, afraid of becoming completely inferior in gun power, they were eventually prompted to build some maximum-size cruisers. The *County* class cruisers all carried eight 8-inch guns; but the *York* class had six 8-inch guns and subsequent cruisers, with the exception of the *Dido* class, carried 6-inch guns. The British, with both European and Pacific commitments in mind, opted for numbers rather than for having a few very powerful ships.

German shipbuilding policy in the late 1920s indicated a preference for powerful commerce-raiders. The *Leipzig* and the *Köln* class carried powerful 5·9-inch armaments within the 6,000-ton limit imposed in 1919 by the Treaty

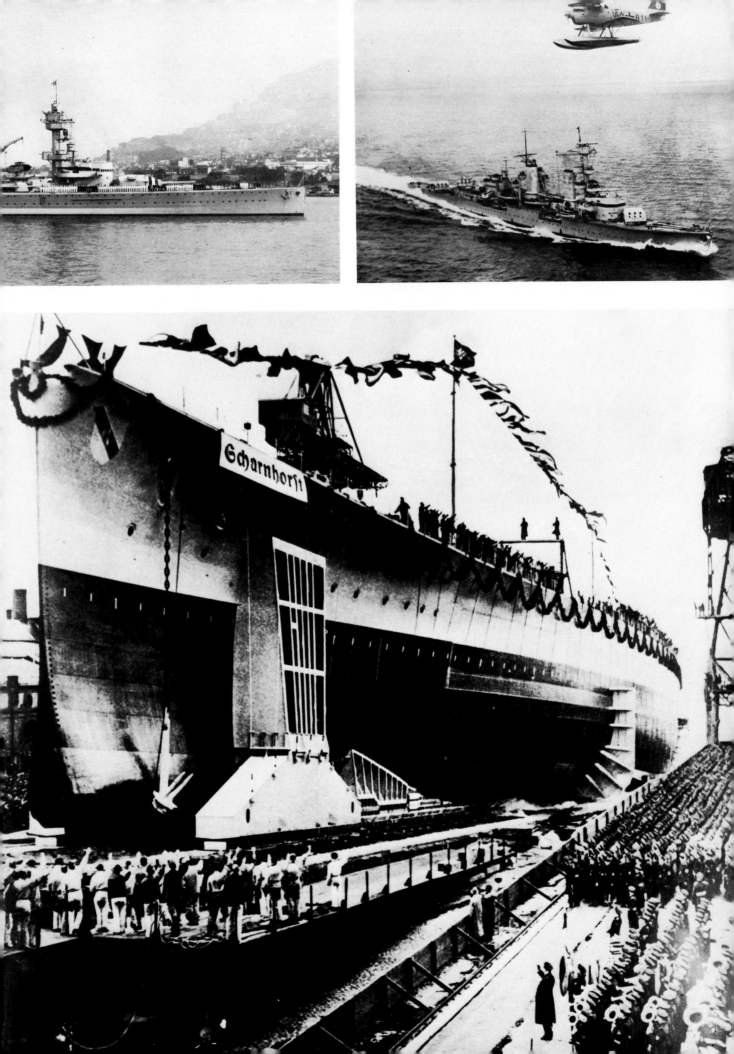

BELOW *The German ship*
Königsberg *fires a salvo*
while on exercises, c.*1930.*
BOTTOM *HMS* Crusader, *a C*
class destroyer, taking part in
combined fleet exercises.
RIGHT *Crowds greet the*

Schleswig Holstein *in 1939.*
She was one of two pre-
dreadnoughts that the
Germans were allowed to
keep after World War I.
INSET *A Japanese destroyer*
in 1942.

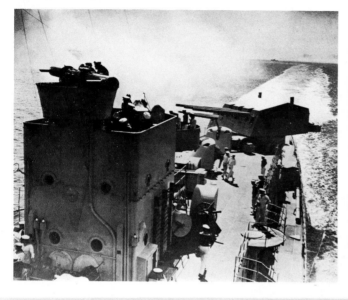

of Versailles. In the 1930s the British responded with the *Leander* class, which had eight 6-inch guns, and the *Southampton* and *Belfast* classes. The latter carried 12 6-inch guns and had an armour belt theoretically capable of standing up to 8-inch gun fire.

Protection was never a priority of Italian design. Speed, though, was a permanent fetish, and the Washington Treaty cruisers were no exception. The *Trento* had a top speed of over 36 knots and the *Zara* made 34 knots – about the same speed as Italy's latest battleship.

In 1929 the first of a new type of cruiser was laid down by Germany. Under the Treaty of Versailles Germany could replace ships over 20 years old but capital ships were not to exceed 10,000 tons. The new cruiser, the *Deutschland*, was called a pocket battleship and was in the capital ship class, but she was designed for commerce-raiding. The three ships of this class exceeded their limitation figure by 1,700 tons despite weight-saving devices. Triple turrets carried six 11-inch guns, which were capable of a broadside of 4,020 pounds at 30,000 yards. Her diesel engines produced 27 knots, which meant she could outrun all but a few ships and outshoot any Washington Treaty cruiser. Her 3,280-ton fuel capacity gave her a 10,000-mile radius at 20 knots.

In light surface craft the needs of Britain differed substantially from those of Japan and the USA. The Japanese and Americans were more interested in fleet destroyers than in the destroyer escorts, sloops and corvettes which were of great importance to the British. After 1937 British construction was increasingly slanted towards sloops and corvettes (and after 1940 towards frigates, which were enlarged oceanic corvettes); all these types were smaller, cheaper and quicker to build than destroyers. Although sloops and corvettes were slower than destroyers this was no great disadvantage because the performance of Asdic fell away at speeds above 20 knots. Furthermore, these ships were more manoeuvrable and had smaller turning circles than destroyers – important considerations when hunting submarines. Their anti-aircraft and anti-submarine capabilities were in fact superior to those of destroyers, for the latter were designed with emphasis on speed, gunnery and torpedo armament.

Most of Britain's destroyer construction was to a standard 1,300-ton displacement until 1935. But because the Americans and Japanese were building much larger and more powerful ships, the British were forced to follow suit. The result was the *Tribal* class: these ships displaced 1,900 tons and doubled the main and AA armaments of previous classes – though at a corresponding cost to the torpedo armament. Unfortunately the *Tribals* were too expensive to be repeated and subsequent classes were smaller and had something like the old balance of armament. The *J* and *K* classes were unique because their longitudinal construction and a reduction in the number of boilers meant that they had single funnels; the *L* class was the first to have dual-purpose guns.

At the outbreak of the Pacific War, the US Navy had 171 destroyers in service of which 100 had been built after 1932. The remainder were World War I vintage and of the 'flush-deck' variety, 50 of which were sold to Britain in 1940. The modern destroyers conformed to a basic 5-inch gun and torpedo-tube armament; these were carried centre-line. The most important single factor about these destroyers was that, beginning with the *Gridley* class, American destroyers, which already had a very long range of 9,000 miles at 15 knots, were able to refuel at sea. From the mid-1930s onwards the Americans were breaking away from a land-based fleet in favour of a navy supported by a fleet train.

Japanese destroyers were, not unnaturally, very similar to their US contemporaries. Those built after World War I carried 4·7-inch guns (the same 47-pounder weapon carried in the British *V* and *W* classes). Later the larger destroyers carried a 5-inch gun but the *Type B* destroyers, though they displaced 2,700 tons, carried 3·9-inch guns. This very powerful gun had a high rate of fire and outranged the contemporary American 5-inch weapon.

Japanese submarine construction fell into three categories. In the 1920s Japan built short-ranged craft with a 20-day endurance and a maximum range of about 10,000 miles. During the 1930s longer-ranged craft were built. The *KD-6A* and *KD-6B* classes had a 45-day range with a 14,000-mile radius of action; this was subsequently increased with the *J-2* and the *J-3* class, which could operate for two months. The *A-1* type, laid down in 1938, had a 90-day range. During the inter-war period, too, some very long-range submarines were built. A 2,430-ton submarine with a 20,000-mile range was completed under the 1919 Programme, but she was not successful. The development of the *M* class by the Royal Navy prompted the Japanese to build a similar type of craft, i.e. one of long range that could carry a seaplane. The *J-1* class carried a seaplane and had a range of 25,000 miles. Throughout the 1930s there were various Japanese yards building seaplane-carrying submarines, but with the passing of time their popularity was eroded; an important factor was that the aircraft could only be used at a cost of imperilling the parent vessel. This did not stop the construction, during World War II, of the super *STo* class. These were the largest conventionally powered submarines ever built; displacement exceeded 6,500 tons and their range was 37,000 miles. They carried three seaplanes and were intended for a raid against the Panama Canal – which never in fact took place.

In virtually every aspect of her equipment, the Imperial Japanese Navy was very powerful at the outbreak of World War II. Her naval aviation and carrier force, though smaller than that of the Americans, was of extremely high quality and had combat experience; the lighter craft were also formidable though, alas for the Japanese, deficient in numbers. But, irrespective of ranges, speeds and gun armament, the most impressive aspect of Japanese destroyers, cruisers and submarines (and their aircraft) was their torpedo armament. In 1933 the *Type 33* torpedo entered service: this was the famous Long Lance, a weapon infinitely superior to anything the British and Americans possessed. Driven by oxygen and leaving no track, it had a 25-mile range at 36 knots and a 49-knot speed over $13\frac{1}{2}$ miles. British and American torpedoes, by comparison, could make 46 knots over $2\frac{1}{2}$ miles or 30 knots over 6·25 miles; their warheads were not more than 320 kilograms against the 500-kg warhead carried by the Japanese weapon.

Japanese surface units, which were intensively trained for night fighting, had a quick-reloading device – something unknown in Western navies. In quality, the Imperial Japanese Navy was probably the best of the major navies; there were, however, some strange lapses in the Japanese conduct of operations. The most notable was their failure to use their submarines in an anti-commerce role, a failure that brought heavy losses when, instead, the submarines attacked strongly defended fighting fleets; in this way the Japanese never achieved the widespread dispersal of American warships that, from the outset, was their aim.

Japanese J *class submarine.* OPPOSITE *Depth-charging from HMS* Skate.

WORLD WAR II

The Balance of Power at Sea, 1939–41

Germany, France and Britain were at war from September 1939; Italy entered the war the following year. In June 1941 the Soviet Union was invaded by Germany and in December the war was extended into the Pacific following Japanese attacks on Pearl Harbor and on European possessions in the Far East.

CATEGORY	GERMANY	FRANCE	BRITAIN	ITALY	USSR	JAPAN	USA
Battleships	2*	6	12	6	3	10	17
Battlecruisers	2	—	3	—	—	—	—
Seaplane carriers	—	1	2	1	—	3	—
Aircraft carriers	—	1	7	—	—	10	7
Heavy cruisers	4*	7	15	7	1	18	18
Light cruisers	5	12	47	12	9	18	19
Destroyers	17	70	159	61	59	113	171
Escorts	8	—	38	83	—	—	—
Submarines	57	77	38	98	?	63	112

* Pre-dreadnoughts.

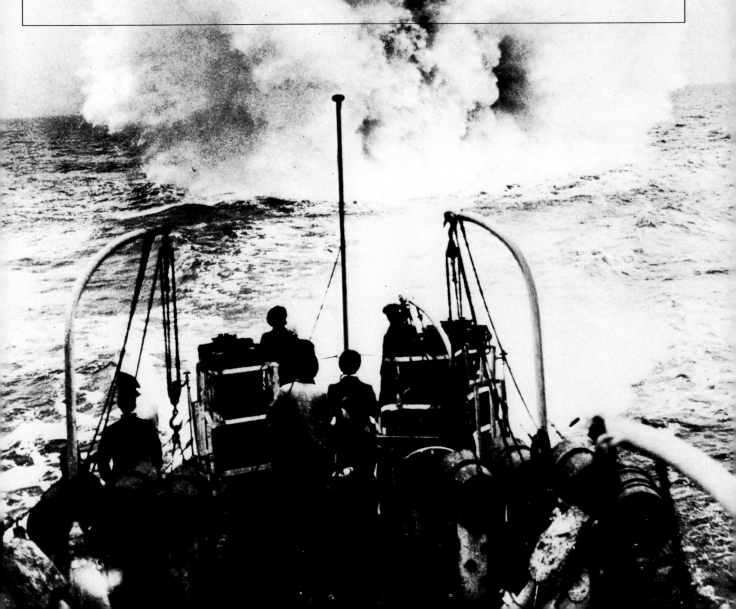

The War at Sea, 1939-1945

A Chronology

THE SYMBOL ☐ DENOTES ACTIVITY OVER A PERIOD OF TIME

1939

SEPTEMBER
1   Germany invades Poland.
3   Britain and France declare war on Germany.
7   First oceanic convoy (Britain to Gibraltar); first transatlantic convoy sails on 15th.
12   US Navy organizes 'neutrality patrols'.

OCTOBER
10   First attempt by Germans to implement wolf-pack tactics.
13   HM battleship *Royal Oak* lost in Scapa Flow.
17   Luftwaffe attacks on Scapa Flow.

NOVEMBER
4   Repeal of US Neutrality Law; materials of war sold to Britain on cash-and-carry basis.

DECEMBER
13   River Plate engagement; *Graf Spee* scuttles herself on 17th.

1940

FEBRUARY
15   Restrictions lifted on German submarine movements.

APRIL
9   German occupation of Denmark; landings at six cities in Norway.
10   German cruiser *Königsberg* becomes first major unit to be sunk by air action; First Battle of Narvik; Second Battle on 13th.
15   Start of Allied landings in Norway.

MAY
10   German invasion of Benelux countries and France.
26   Start of Dunkirk evacuation (Operation Dynamo); completed on 4 June.

JUNE
4   Start of Allied evacuation from Norway; completed on 10th.
8   HM aircraft carrier *Glorious* sunk by battlecruisers *Scharnhorst* and *Gneisenau*.

22   France concludes an armistice.
☐   Allied monthly shipping losses pass 500,000 tons for first time.

JULY
3   British attack French fleet at Oran.
16   Hitler issues directive for plan to invade Britain (Operation Sea Lion).
19   US emergency programme authorizes 1,325,000 tons of warship construction.

SEPTEMBER
17   Operation Sea Lion indefinitely postponed after failure of Luftwaffe to defeat RAF.
27   Axis pact signed in Berlin by Germany, Italy and Japan.

OCTOBER
28   Italians invade Greece.

NOVEMBER
11   Naval aircraft cripple Italian battle fleet in Taranto harbour.

1941

MARCH
11   Passing of Lend Lease Act by USA.
30   Battle off Cape Matapan.

MAY
15   US Navy takes over Argentia naval base in Canada.
20   German airborne invasion of Crete.
27   German battleship *Bismarck* sunk after a 9-day sortie during which she sank HM battlecruiser *Hood* (24th). Start of Allied evacuation of Crete; completed on 31st.

JUNE
22   Germany invades USSR (Operation Barbarossa).

JULY
7   US forces relieve British garrison in Iceland; first US convoy sails to Iceland.
26   USA freezes all Japanese assets and institutes oil embargo.

SEPTEMBER
16   US warships form convoy escorts for first time; first clashes with German

U-boats. German U-boats diverted to Mediterranean.

NOVEMBER
7   US merchant shipping armed and allowed to enter war zones.
14   HM aircraft carrier *Ark Royal* lost.
25   HM battleship *Barham* lost.

DECEMBER
7   Japanese attack Pearl Harbor, Malaya and Siam (Thailand).
8   USA declares war.
10   Japanese invade Philippines.

1942

JANUARY
11   Japan invades Dutch East Indies: territory capitulates on 8 March.
13   Start of German submarine campaign off east coast of USA.

FEBRUARY
12   Escape from Brest to Germany of *Scharnhorst* and *Gneisenau*.
15   Fall of Singapore to Japanese forces.
27   Battle of Java Sea.

MARCH
28   Normandie Lock at St Nazaire destroyed.
☐   Total of 273 Allied merchant ships lost, mostly in Far East.

APRIL
8   Capitulation of Philippines (except Corregidor, 6 May).
18   Doolittle raid on Tokyo.

MAY
4-8   Battle of Coral Sea brings first check to Japanese advance.

JUNE
4-6   Battle of Midway.
☐   Highest monthly shipping losses of war – 834,196 tons (including PQ17 disaster).

AUGUST
7   US Landings on Guadalcanal: island not cleared until Japanese evacuations in February 1943.
19   Dieppe Raid.

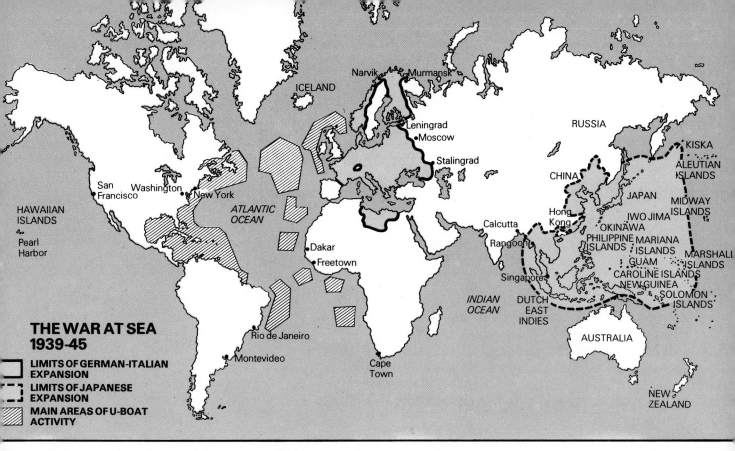

THE WAR AT SEA 1939-45

LIMITS OF GERMAN-ITALIAN EXPANSION

LIMITS OF JAPANESE EXPANSION

MAIN AREAS OF U-BOAT ACTIVITY

SEPTEMBER

☐ Japanese land offensive in New Guinea halted by Australians.

NOVEMBER

4 Axis forces defeated at El Alamein.

8 Anglo–American landings in North Africa (Operation Torch).

20 Siege of Malta lifted.

27 French fleet at Toulon scuttles itself to prevent German take-over.

1943

MARCH

16-20 Biggest convoy battle of war in North Atlantic.

☐ Air gap in North Atlantic closed; Arctic convoys suspended.

APRIL

7-11 Collapse of Japanese air offensive against Marshall Islands.

MAY

13 Fall of Tunis.

☐ Decisive defeat of German U-boats: 37 sunk in North Atlantic.

JUNE

☐ U-boats withdraw from North Atlantic.

30 US landings on New Georgia.

JULY

10 Allied landings in Sicily.

AUGUST

3 Start of German evacuation of Sicily; completed on 17th.

SEPTEMBER

3 Allied landings on mainland Italy.

8 Italian armistice; Italian fleet surrenders on 10th.

OCTOBER

☐ German U-boat offensive resumed and defeated; 26 submarines sunk.

NOVEMBER

1 US landings on Bougainville; Tarawa invaded on 20th.

DECEMBER

26 *Scharnhorst* sunk off North Cape.

1944

JANUARY

22 Allied landings at Anzio.

MAY

☐ Snorkel comes into general use.

JUNE

6 Allied invasion of Normandy.

18-21 Battle of Philippine Sea.

JULY

21 US landings on Guam.

AUGUST

15 Allied landings in south of France.

SEPTEMBER

☐ Start of German submarine campaign in British coastal waters.

OCTOBER

20 US landings at Leyte; first *kamikaze* attacks next day.

NOVEMBER

1 Walcheren assault; Scheldt estuary cleared for Allied use.

12 German battleship *Tirpitz* sunk by RAF Bomber Command.

22 Formation of British Pacific Fleet.

DECEMBER

8 Start of US pre-invasion bombardment of Iwo Jima.

1945

JANUARY

☐ German U-boat *Type XXIII* becomes operational.

9 US landings on Luzon; cleared in June.

FEBRUARY

16 First carrier raids on Japan since 1942 Doolittle Raid.

19 US landings on Iwo Jima; cleared 23 March.

APRIL

☐ German U-boat *Type XXI* becomes operational.

1 US landings on Okinawa; cleared 21 June.

7 Japanese battleship *Yamato* sunk.

MAY

2 British landings at Rangoon.

4 U-boats recalled to Germany.

8 Unconditional German surrender.

JULY

14 First coastal bombardment of Japan.

AUGUST

6 Atomic bombing of Hiroshima.

8 USSR declares war on Japan.

9 Atomic bombing of Nagasaki.

14 Japanese government indicates willingness to surrender.

SEPTEMBER

2 Japanese instrument of surrender signed aboard US battleship *Missouri* in Tokyo Bay.

Chapter Six
World War II

This war marked the eclipse of two institutions whose supremacy had been constant factors for over two centuries. Between 1941 and 1945 the US Navy, backed by almost unlimited resources, finally relegated the Royal Navy to a position of inferiority; this, but for the Washington Treaty, would have happened earlier. Also during this period, the battleship lost its place as queen of the seas and arbiter of naval conflict.

From early in the war, in Norway and at Dunkirk, it became obvious that surface vessels could not operate in waters controlled by enemy aircraft, yet only gradually did changes of attitude occur concerning the relative balance between gun and aircraft. In 1939 the battleship was still supreme, the aircraft merely an extension of its guns. The aircraft was for reconnaissance: it was to spot for the guns, provide air defence and make attacks on a fleeing enemy with the object of delivering prey to a pursuing battle fleet.

To the British, faced with enemies who lacked carriers, such concepts were both sensible and successful. At Oran, in 1940, aircraft spotted for the guns of the battle fleet and carried out torpedo attacks on the French fleet; in 1941 enemies in retreat were destroyed by surface units after having been crippled by air strikes – at the battle off Cape Matapan and in the chasing of the *Bismarck*. Yet all the while the power of the aircraft, in terms both of endurance and detecting ability, and also the power of its torpedoes were growing at rates faster than the battleship's defensive power, which had reached its zenith.

Designers improved the defensive power of battleships: beam size increased, bulkheading grew in intricacy and there was a massive increase in anti-aircraft firepower; but such innovations did not save the battleship. When commissioned, the monster Japanese battleship *Yamato* carried a secondary armament of 12 (4 × 3) 6·1-inch guns and an anti-aircraft defence of 12 (6 × 2) 5-inch guns, 24 (8 × 3) 25-mm and 4 (2 × 2) 13-mm guns. When she sailed on her last mission, her main armament was equipped with a special AA shell which contained 6,000 rounds of 25-mm bullets fired on a time fuse, like a shotgun, to a

In World War II aircraft held the key to mobility at sea.
OPPOSITE, ABOVE *In May 1940 German bombs fall around the British troopship* Mashobra *in Harstadt harbour, Norway.*
RIGHT *The Japanese attack on Pearl Harbor, 7 December 1941. In the centre, surrounded by a huge cloud of smoke, is the* Arizona, *which was sunk. To the left are the* West Virginia *and the* Tennessee, *both of which suffered severe damage.*

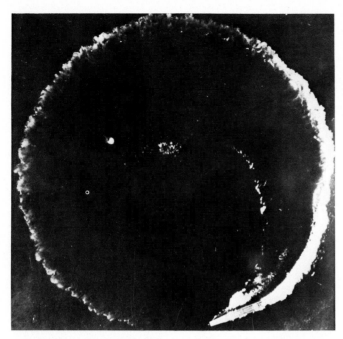

maximum range of 30,000 yards. Half her 6·1-inch guns had been suppressed; instead she carried 24 (12 × 2) 5-inch and 146 (40 × 3 and 26 × 1) 25-mm anti-aircraft guns. Such defences, however, proved inadequate. Intercepted by US naval aircraft on a one-way sortie to help relieve Okinawa in April 1945, she was quickly sunk; her massive banks of anti-aircraft guns failed to make up for a lack of air cover.

British and American capital ships also increased their anti-aircraft armament, but never to the extent of the Japanese. The *Duke of York*, for example, in addition to her original armament of 16 (8 × 2) 5·25-inch dual-purpose guns (which had a rate of fire of 18 rounds per minute) and 48 (6 × 8) 2-pounder AA guns, was given another 40 (2 × 8 and 6 × 4) 2-pounder, 8 (2 × 4) 40-mm and 16 (8 × 2) 20-mm anti-aircraft guns. Yet the survival of battleships could not be guaranteed by their own guns and powers of resistance. At Taranto and Pearl Harbor, aircraft unmistakeably showed their ability to sink capital ships; and on 10 December 1941 HMS *Repulse* became the first capital ship to be sunk by aircraft whilst on the open sea. If gunned capital ships were still to operate, they now had to do so only after air supremacy was assured or they had to be accompanied by carriers that were prepared to fight for and secure command of the air.

Thus during the war the battleship was relegated to secondary duties: pre-invasion bombardment, convoy protection, the provision of anti-aircraft defence for carriers and to act as their last line of defence in the event of a surface attack. Battleships were also used for special operations such as the movement of gold and key personnel. The carrier took over as the major strike weapon. In the Pacific, it did so immediately after Pearl Harbor, when the Americans were bereft of serviceable battleships; to make up for this deficiency, the concept of the Fast Carrier Force was devised.

ABOVE LEFT *The Japanese carrier* Soryu *circles as she tries to avoid the bombs of American B-17s at the Battle of Midway, June 1942.* ABOVE AND OPPOSITE, ABOVE *A Japanese destroyer is* singled out and blown up by an American B-25 bomber at Ormoc Bay, Leyte. BELOW HMS Repulse *sails from Singapore on her last voyage, 8 December 1941. Two days later she fell*

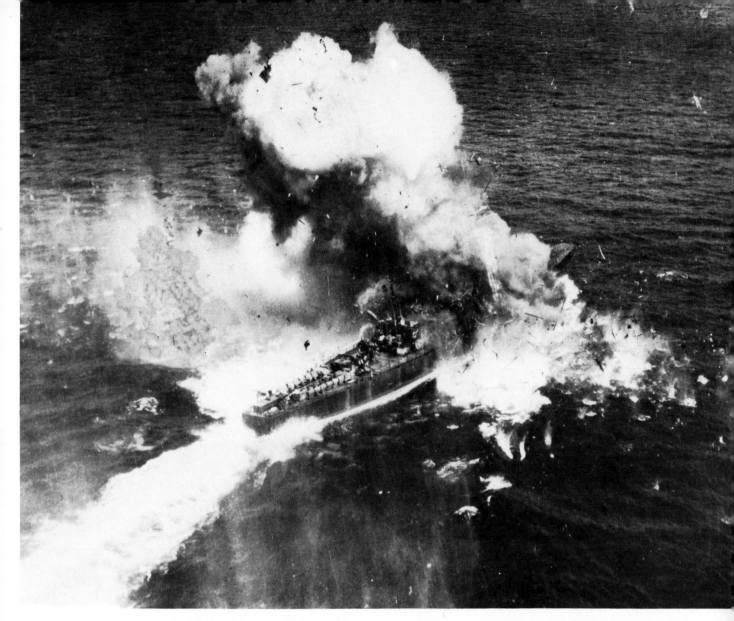

victim to a Japanese air
attack – the first capital ship
to be sunk by aircraft on the
open seas.
RIGHT *A 20-mm Quad anti-
aircraft gun in operation
aboard the German ship*

Prinz Eugen.
BELOW *The 15-inch guns of
HMS* Valiant. *In the
background are the* Barham
and the Warspite, *'steaming'
in line-ahead formation as
they open fire.*

The War in the Pacific

In the six months after Pearl Harbor the Imperial Japanese armed forces ran amok in the Pacific, seizing Malaya, the Philippines and the Dutch East Indies. Their gains were immense; even so, behind the conquests there was neither the manpower, the industrial resources, the merchant fleet nor the fighting ships that the Japanese needed to implement their policy. This was to build defence lines on which the enemy would expend his strength until he tired of war and accepted a negotiated peace.

Japanese policy depended entirely on the survival of the Imperial battle fleet, which was to operate on internal lines of communication and there meet and defeat American counter-attacks. But in the Battle of Midway (June 1942) the Japanese lost four of the six large carriers with which they had started the war. During 1942 American losses were equally severe, but there was one important difference: the Japanese could not replace their lost pilots, aircraft and carriers at the same rate as the Americans and therefore had to contend, as time went by, with a growing inferiority.

In 1943 the Americans replaced their losses from the year before with the first of the *Essex* class carriers. These ships displaced 27,000 tons and could steam at 32 knots. For defence they carried 12 5-inch and up to 68 40-mm AA guns. An extreme beam of $147\frac{1}{2}$ feet incorporated for the first time an outboard lift and an overhanging flight-deck to port; ships of this class could carry 100 aircraft. Unlike British carriers, the American ships at this time did not have armoured flight-decks and hangars. They were, nevertheless, extremely rugged and although many were hit and some extensively damaged, none was sunk.

In time the Americans also came to appreciate the value of defensive armour. The *Midway* class, built during the war but commissioned too late for active service against Japan, had an armoured flight-deck; this was not, moreover, included at the expense of speed or offensive power. These ships, displacing 45,000 tons, could carry 137 aircraft. Increased displacement was in fact central to the *Midway* class's great carrying ability, and it was also favoured by the British, who were working from the other end of the equation; their ships already had a strong defensive arrangement but needed greater striking power.

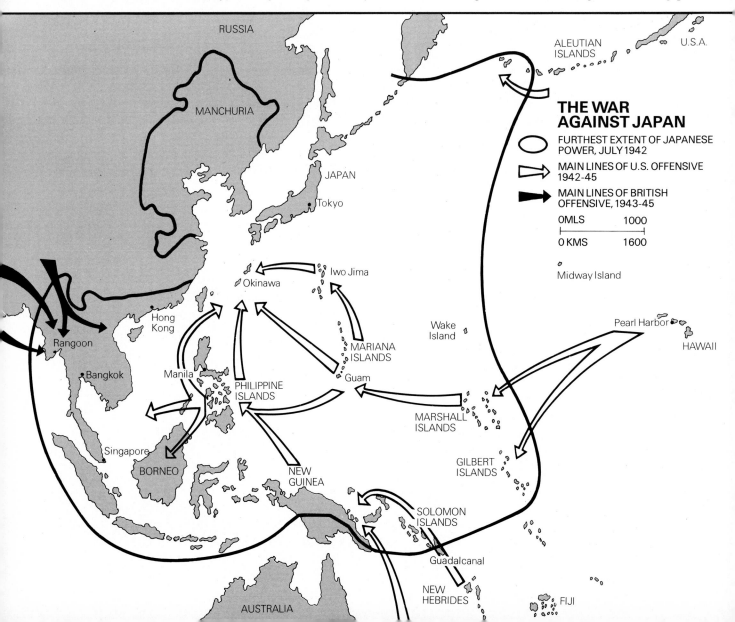

THE WAR AGAINST JAPAN

FURTHEST EXTENT OF JAPANESE POWER, JULY 1942

MAIN LINES OF U.S. OFFENSIVE 1942-45

MAIN LINES OF BRITISH OFFENSIVE, 1943-45

0 MLS   1000
0 KMS   1600

ABOVE *A panoramic view of the chaos at Pearl Harbor. Around the black cloud in the centre, emanating chiefly from the stricken USS* Arizona, *are smaller black puffs of smoke from the American AA guns which accounted for 28 Japanese aircraft. The smaller clouds to the left mark where the* Shaw *and a floating dock were hit.*
BELOW *The art of naval camouflage. The USS* New Orleans *lies concealed beneath a mass of netting and foliage at Tulagi after losing a section of her bow in the Battle of Tassafaronga, 30 November 1942*

In October 1942 the first of the new *Audacious* class was laid down and it was anticipated that these 36,000-ton ships would be the Royal Navy's first carriers to operate 100 aircraft; this however, turned out to be an unrealized dream.

In the war in the Pacific it was the *Essex* class carriers that spearheaded the American victory. Using radar and improved aircraft that gave them a considerable material advantage over the Japanese, these carriers quickly eliminated enemy air and sea strength in the South Pacific. Thrusting through the Carolines and Marianas, the US Navy provoked the Japanese to fight and lose the Battle of the Philippine Sea in July 1944 – the first carrier battle for two years. In this engagement the Japanese lost three carriers and most of their aircraft and crews. Thus devoid of cover, the Philippines were invaded and conquered despite a despairing sortie by the Imperial Japanese Navy, which was crushed in the Battle of Leyte Gulf. Ranging over the Philippines, the Ryukus, Indo–China, the Chinese coast, Formosa and finally the Japanese

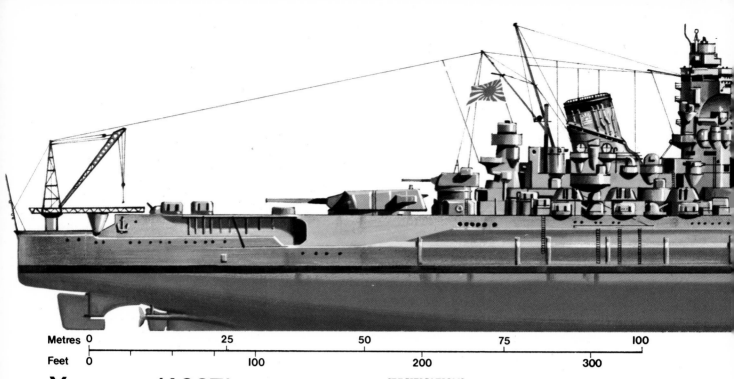

Metres 0   25   50   75   100

Feet 0   100   200   300

Yamato (1937)

In World War II the Imperial Japanese Navy acquired two monster battleships, the *Yamato* and her sister ship *Musashi*. They were the largest battleships ever built. On these pages the *Yamato* is seen at different stages in her development; in her brief career her anti-aircraft armament was progressively strengthened from 24 25-mm machine guns to a final total of 146. She entered service in February 1942 and served in the Pacific theatre until she was caught, on 6 April 1945, in a massed attack by carrier-borne aircraft. Although immensely strong she was unable to withstand a bombardment that in the space of two hours registered seven bomb and 12 torpedo hits, and she blew up and sank.

SPECIFICATIONS

Displacement	64,000 tons
Length	863 feet
Beam	127 feet
Draught	35 feet
Armament	9 18-inch guns
(when completed)	12 6·1-inch guns
	12 5-inch guns
	24 25-mm AA guns
	4 13-mm guns
	6 aircraft
Armour	16 inch belt
Engines	150,000 hp; steam turbines
Speed	27 knots

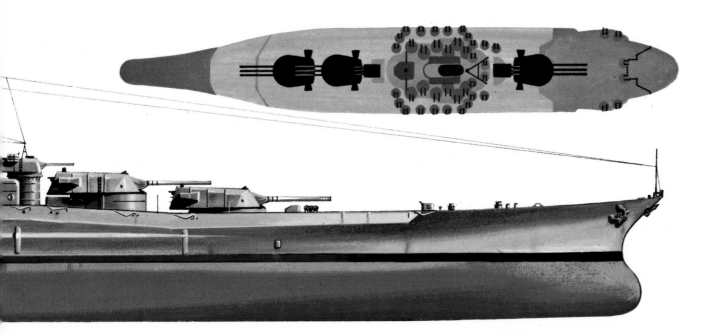

RIGHT *The after flight deck, from where the* Yamato's *floatplanes (Aichi 'Jakes' and Mitsubishi 'Petes') were catapulted aloft.*

BELOW *An American LSM (Landing Ship Medium) fires off a battery of rockets.*
BOTTOM *US Navy landing craft bring essential supplies to back up the troops engaged in the struggle for Iwo Jima.*
RIGHT *Surviving Japanese sailors prepare to take to the water as their destroyer is about to sink, shattered in a raid by the US 345th Bomber Group.*

homeland itself, the carrier aircraft cleared the seas of the enemy merchant and fighting ships that remained; and provided air defence for the battleships when they started their bombardment of the Japanese coast in July 1945.

By the time that the atomic bombs were dropped, Japan was at the end of her tether. Her Navy had virtually ceased to exist and her Army had been defeated in most theatres. Economically, too, her position was desperate: her people were on the brink of starvation and her factories were drastically under-supplied. The vital supply lines that brought food and raw materials to Japan and took troops and supplies to the theatres of war had been severed; the Japanese merchant fleet had been all but annihilated. In 1941 Japan had needed 10,000,000 tons of shipping a year to maintain herself, of which her own fleet could carry only six millions, the balance having to be carried in foreign-owned ships. Yet, excluding any that she could capture, four million tons of foreign shipping was lost to Japan as soon as she went to war.

In December 1941, with no other means of taking the fight to the enemy, the Americans launched unrestricted submarine warfare. Operating mainly from Hawaii until early 1945, when the submarine base was moved to Guam, US submarines sank 1,153 merchant ships totalling 4,889,000 tons at a cost of 52 of their own number. Japan was able to sustain her losses until November 1943. After that date she was compelled, in her efforts to reinforce

island garrisons under attack, to send merchant ships into waters controlled by US air and naval forces; there the merchant ships took losses that Japan's limited construction facilities could not replace.

Many of the reasons for this state of affairs lay in the technical inferiority of Japanese equipment as compared to that of the USA. Whereas, for example, Japanese aircraft showed relatively little improvement during the course of the war, American aircraft improved out of all recognition and ultimately outclassed the Japanese. And while, in the submarine war, Japanese units lacked radar, throughout 1943 American submarines were being equipped with the new and very effective SJ sets. The Japanese also lacked a means of locating the High Frequency voice radios used by the submarines. Nor, in the strategic field, did they aid their own cause by their attitude towards convoys: initially reluctant to adopt the system at all, when they finally did so their escorts were fatally weak. Instead they preferred to mount offensive patrols just as the British had done in the Great War – and with an equal lack of success. These weaknesses in numbers and in the quality of their equipment were critical deficiencies that cost Japan the battle of the sea lanes. In nature, however, they were not dissimilar to weaknesses experienced by the British and Americans in the Atlantic, but which those powers managed to remedy before this struggle reached its climax in the spring of 1943.

Essex Class Carriers

The fleet carriers of the *Essex* class were a decisive force in the Pacific theatre. Arriving in 1943, they spearheaded the US offensive through the Carolinas and Marianas, their commanders using their technological superiority in terms both of the ships themselves and of their more powerful aircraft to batter a path to within reach of the Japanese homeland. The *Essex* carriers were tough ships, even though, unlike their British counterparts, their flight-decks and hangars were not armoured. They were big ships, too, with room for 100 aircraft; and their design included an outboard elevator.

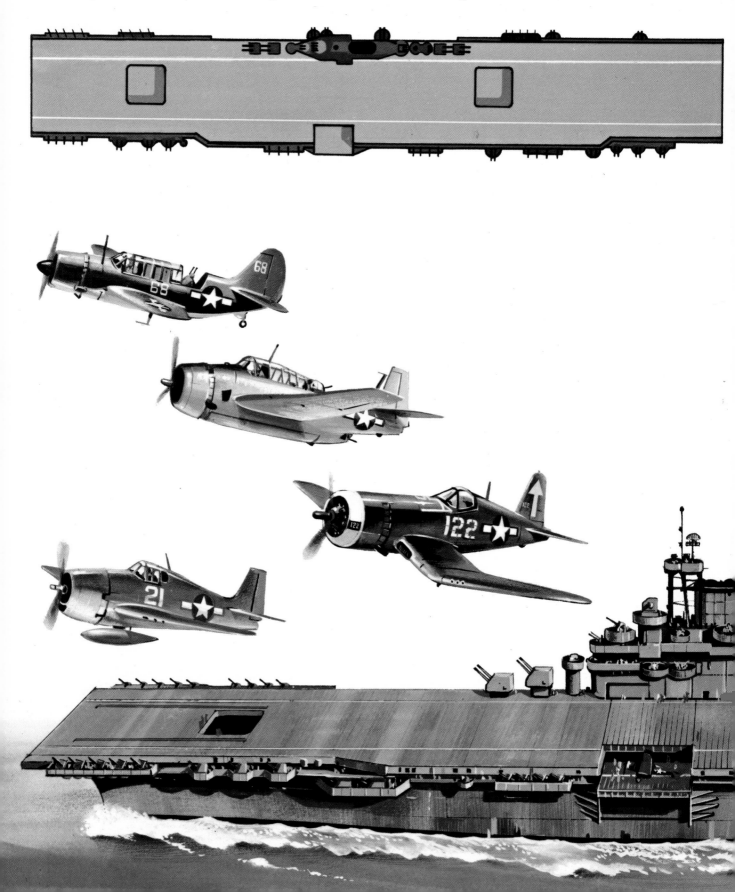

FAR LEFT AND BELOW The representative ship on these pages is the *Essex*, first of the new class. She was laid down in April 1941 and completed in December the following year. Dimensions, etc., vary among the 20 ships of the class that were built in wartime, but those of the *Essex* were as follows:

Displacement	27,000 tons
Length	820 feet
Beam (extreme)	147 feet 6 inches
Draught	20 feet
Armament	12×5 inch guns
	40×40 mm AA guns
	50×20 mm guns
	(quadruple mounts)
Armour (max.)	2-3 inches (side amidships)
Engines	150,000 hp; geared turbines
Carrier capacity	100 aircraft
Speed	32 knots

LEFT *Shown here are four of the carrier-borne aircraft associated with* Essex *carriers in World War II. The top illustration is of the Curtiss SB2C Helldiver, a dive-bomber which entered service in November 1943; it had a maximum speed in the SB2C-3 model of 294 mph and was armed with two 20-mm cannon, one ·5-inch machine gun, and up to 1,000 pounds of bombs or one*

torpedo carried internally; maximum range was 1,925 miles. Second is the Grumman TBM Avenger, one of the war's most successful torpedo bombers. It had a speed of 270 mph and a range of 1,020 miles; armament consisted of five machine guns and up to 2,000 pounds of bombs, one 1,920-pound torpedo or eight rockets. The third aircraft shown is a Chance Vought F4U-1D

Corsair fighter bomber, a variant in the powerful Corsair series of naval fighters; in the F4U-4 version these aircraft could achieve a maximum speed of 446 mph. The bottom aircraft is a Grumman F6F-3 Hellcat fighter; these were a scaled-up and more powerful version of the earlier Wildcat; armament was six ·5-inch machine guns, top speed 375 mph and range 1,090 miles.

ABOVE *The USS* Intrepid, *an Essex class carrier laid down in December 1941, here seen after major conversion work completed in 1957 had given her an angled flight deck, steam catapult and an enclosed bow.*

The Battle of the Atlantic

In the European context the war at sea was, in the absence of a strong German surface fleet and a determined Italian navy, a struggle conducted along the sea lanes by German submarines against Britain's trade. Initially, the German submarines operated under two handicaps. Firstly, war had come too early, at a time when only 57 craft were available instead of the 300 that in the Germans' estimation was the number needed if they were to bring Britain to her knees; and, secondly, even that small number was restricted in its operations. On the other hand Britain, with 20,000,000 tons of shipping, offered many weakly defended targets: indeed, she went to war with a mere 87 escort vessels of which only 26 were in the Western Approaches. Furthermore, most of these escorts lacked the range to protect merchantmen more than a few hundred miles west of Ireland. This was so because the British had neglected to build up between the wars a fleet train that could replenish ships at sea (it was not until 1942 that the practice of refuelling at sea became widespread in the Royal Navy).

In the early days convoys were protected not by ships that had been trained to work together but by those that were available at the time; in such a situation numbers were more important than teamwork, technique and training. The consequences were entirely predictable. In 1940 the Germans lost 23 U-boats, in 1941 35 and in 1942 87. But against these figures must be put those of a strenuous

building programme: in the last quarter of 1941 alone 69 new submarines were commissioned and in January 1942 U-boat strength stood at 249, of which 90 were operational. Britain's merchant shipping losses in 1940 and 1941 were about 4,000,000 tons in each year – more than twice the replacement capacity.

However, losses were considerably reduced in the North Atlantic between July and December 1941, when the monthly average was only about 100,000 tons. The principal reason for this drop lay in the improved defences of the convoys; and, partly as a result of the tightening-up by the British, U-boats began to be moved away from the area. British corvettes with a transatlantic capability were increasing in numbers, and sloops of the *Black Swan* class were diverted from other theatres to the North Atlantic. A further improvement was that the new escorts were being trained as groups – in the hope, of course, that they would be kept together and not be squandered piecemeal. In addition, U-boats were losing their invulnerability. The increasingly widespread use of radar now gave escorts the

OPPOSITE, ABOVE *A German Type VII-C U-boat in the Arctic Sea north of Norway.*
OPPOSITE, BELOW *A U-boat is attacked with depth charges dropped from a US Army B-25.*
BELOW *The map shows how the air gap narrowed during the war, so inhibiting the relative freedom of the U-boats, and right, U-boat construction in wartime.*

opportunity to counter-attack a surfaced U-boat as it moved in on a convoy; in other words the escorts took up the offensive before, and not after, the enemy could claim any victims.

By an unfortunate chain of consequences, the entry of the United States into the war was initially disastrous for the Allied cause. Following the fall of France, the United States had adopted an increasingly hostile position *vis-à-vis* Germany; in material ways this attitude was demonstrated through the provision of escorts for British convoys and through the declaration of Neutrality Zones off the east coast of America, in which shipping could move without danger. But when the Axis Powers declared war on the United States, the hitherto protected ships lost their invulnerability. The result was a slaughter of American shipping in the first six months of 1942. In that year 1,006 ships were sunk in the North Atlantic and submarines accounted for 1,160 Allied ships in all theatres. The total Allied losses, from all causes and in all theatres, was a staggering 1,664 ships totalling 7,800,000 tons. The winter months brought some relief to the Allies but in March 1943, despite increasing escort strength, the U-boats achieved their third highest total of monthly sinkings in the war (627,377 tons), and it seemed that Britain might be defeated despite the convoy system and American resources.

However, in the summer of 1943 the submarine challenge was not simply beaten back but decisively defeated. Despite

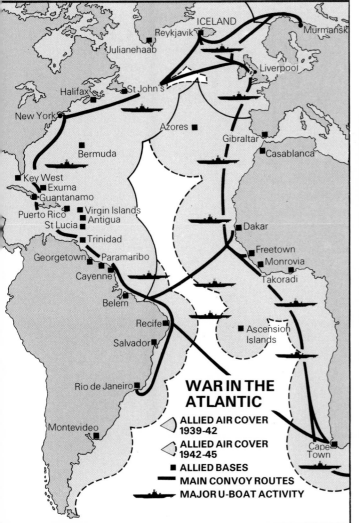

WAR IN THE ATLANTIC

◁ ALLIED AIR COVER 1939-42
◁ ALLIED AIR COVER 1942-45
■ ALLIED BASES
▬ MAIN CONVOY ROUTES
⚓ MAJOR U-BOAT ACTIVITY

Destroyer   Corvette   Merchantmen   Asdic coverage in 160° arc,
range 2,500 yards

Convoy
Commodore

the high rate of sinkings in March, the Germans were now failing to destroy ships faster than the Allies could build replacements. Mainly because of the mass production techniques of the American yards, construction was running at 8,800,000 tons a year in the last quarter of 1942; a year later the rate of building had almost doubled (16,400,000 tons). In the first quarter of 1943 building exceeded losses for the first time since 1939, and the Germans were subsequently unable to reverse this trend.

Nor were they able to maintain their high rate of sinkings. Better convoy protection ensured more safe arrivals: in August 1943 only two ships were lost in the North Atlantic and between June 1943 and May 1944 only 442,684 tons

ABOVE *The diagram shows how Atlantic convoys were organized in the early part of the war, in about 1940–41. In those days the escorts' detector equipment was fairly limited in its powers, and crews could not hope to pick up a submerged submarine at* *distances in excess of 1,500 yards.*
ABOVE RIGHT *Dawn breaks over an Atlantic convoy, as seen from USS* Arkansas.
BELOW *The sinking, in June 1941, of the SS* Kemmendine, *blown up by a German torpedo.*

were lost in that theatre. The submarines were forced to more distant and less lucrative waters, away from the vital USA–UK supply route. Increased convoy protection also produced greater success against the U-boats. In the first six months of 1943, 96 submarines were sunk, and 237 in the whole year. At the height of the battle, in May, 41 U-boats failed to return to their pens. Increasing strength, better weapons, and effective co-ordination and teamwork were the simple but indispensable factors behind the Allied success.

Air cover for the convoys was of the utmost importance in the Battle of the Atlantic. In the early years of the war, vast areas of the ocean had been safe for the submarines, but gradually the air gap – the area between Britain and the American continent not covered by air patrols – was cut down. In July 1941, RAF Coastal Command had only one squadron of nine Very Long Range aircraft; two years later there were 105 aircraft in nine squadrons. Long Range aircraft and flying boats similarly increased in numbers. For the first time there were no safe areas for the U-boats to run to on the surface and recharge their batteries. From the middle of 1942 onwards, convoys had their own air cover on an ever-growing scale, and the escort carrier began to appear in force. By October 1943 the British had 25 such ships, nearly all American-built. These redoubtable craft doubled, when necessary, for fleet

carriers and assault carriers during invasions, but their greatest service was in searching for and hunting down submarines in the vicinity of convoys. They displaced about 12,000 tons and carried up to 18 aircraft.

Equally as important as the increasing number of aircraft was their improved equipment. In the summer of 1942 a new 1·5-metre radar set was introduced; this was followed early the next year by the 10-cm set. The latter, to which the Germans failed to find a counter in the critical phase of the battle, allowed aircraft to make contact in extremely bad weather conditions and at night. Combined with new, shallow-pattern depth-charges, which were introduced to aircraft in mid-1942, this equipment was so effective that in 1943 aircraft accounted for 116 submarines.

Surface escorts also increased in numbers and hitting

power. New depth-charges with a 500-foot capability were introduced, and a mortar that could throw 24 contact bombs some 250 yards forwards of the ship entered service at the start of 1943. This mortar was extremely useful because it enabled an attack to be made without losing contact with the submarine, whereas in a depth-charge attack the Asdic lost contact as the range was closed. (Forward-throwing and fast-sinking depth-charges appeared later, towards the end of the war.) In addition, detection devices for locating signalling U-boats began to appear in growing numbers during 1942. All these weapons and detection devices substantially contributed to victory, though in the end the critical factors were the strength and training of the escorts. In October 1943 the Royal Navy disposed of 288 destroyers and escort destroyers and 325 sloops, frigates and corvettes. By the end of the war 257 destroyers (of both types), 50 sloops, 235 frigates and 257 corvettes flew the White Ensign.

Most of this anti-submarine strength was concentrated against the 400 U-boats that remained to Germany at the end of the war; the results of this confrontation were such that, in April 1945, for example, 15 U-boats were sunk in the waters around the British Isles. Interestingly though,

OPPOSITE, ABOVE *An American Liberty ship, one of the mass-produced cargo ships that kept the transatlantic supply lines open; construction in the American yards was such that by the end of 1943 the annual rate was in the order of 16,400,000 tons.*
OPPOSITE, BELOW *The Tirpitz in Narvik-Bogen Fjord in July 1942, surrounded by anti-torpedo netting.*
BELOW *Mechanics at work in the hanger of HMS* Argus.

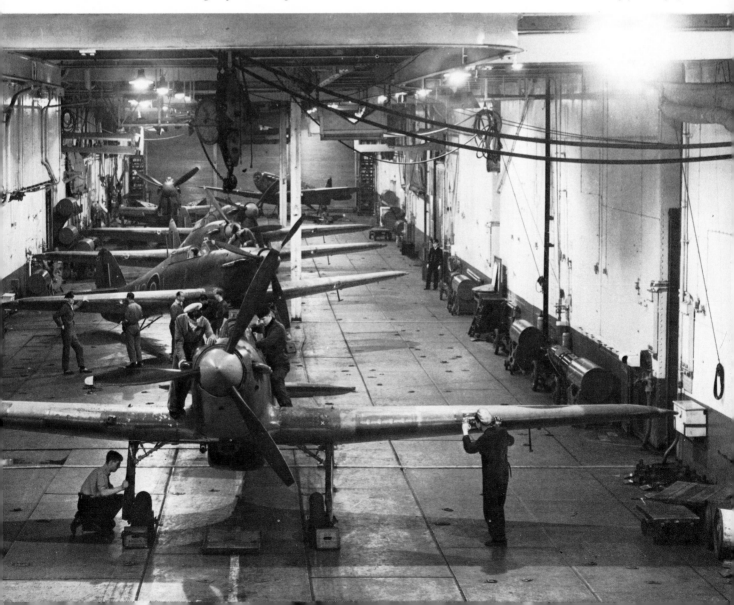

TOP *The type II-B; one of the early, coastal types in service at the beginning of the war, survivors were later kept on for training duties. These U-boats were armed with three 21-inch torpedo tubes and carried six torpedoes or eight mines.*

The U-Boats

On these pages are four of the principal types of U-boat used against Allied shipping in the Atlantic. The campaign opened with dramatic successes for the U-boats and huge losses for the Allies until they learnt successfully to apply the convoy system. The decisive years were 1942–43: in '42 1,006 ships were sunk in the North Atlantic and submarines accounted for 1,160 Allied ships in all theatres; total tonnage lost that year amounted to 7,800,000 tons. But by the end of the year production in the American shipyards was booming, and convoy techniques were being tightened up, with tangible results. In the first quarter of 1943 the rate of Allied building exceeded losses for the first time since 1939. The U-boats were never to recover their supremacy; instead their own losses mounted, thanks to the greater strength of the Allied convoys, their improved weapons, co-ordination and increasingly effective air cover.

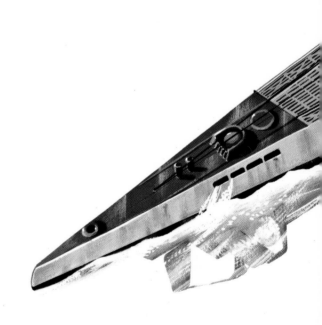

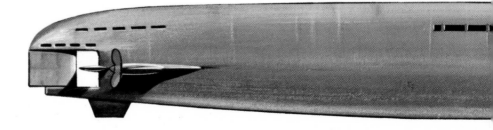

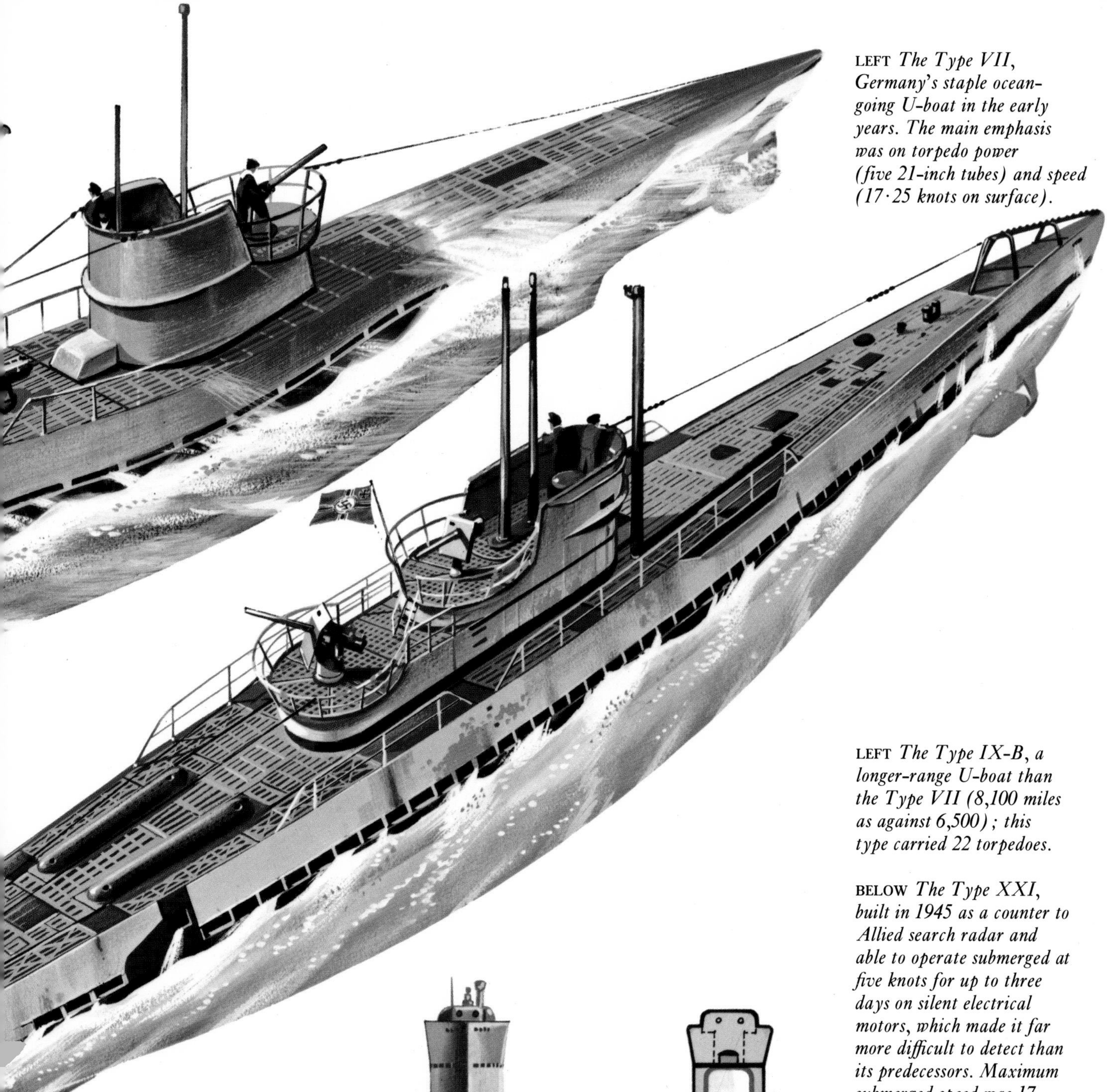

LEFT *The Type VII,
Germany's staple ocean-
going U-boat in the early
years. The main emphasis
was on torpedo power
(five 21-inch tubes) and speed
(17·25 knots on surface).*

LEFT *The Type IX-B, a
longer-range U-boat than
the Type VII (8,100 miles
as against 6,500); this
type carried 22 torpedoes.*

BELOW *The Type XXI,
built in 1945 as a counter to
Allied search radar and
able to operate submerged at
five knots for up to three
days on silent electrical
motors, which made it far
more difficult to detect than
its predecessors. Maximum
submerged speed was 17
knots (for one hour);
armament consisted of 23
torpedoes or 12 torpedoes
and 12 mines with four
AA guns mounted on the
conning tower. The cross-
section view is taken at the
point amidships on the
main illustration.*

ABOVE *A US destroyer lays a smoke screen across the bows of* HMS Enterprise *during the D-Day bombardment, which took place on 6 June 1944.*
RIGHT *With barrage balloons aloft, a procession of Allied landing craft makes the Channel crossing prior to the D-Day invasion of France.*
OPPOSITE, BELOW *The British Force H – the aircraft carrier* Ark Royal *with the* Sheffield *and the* Renown.

all these losses were of submarines of a standard design; no losses were taken by the new types of submarine that were then becoming available. The latter craft in fact enjoyed a remarkable immunity from detection, and hence from destruction.

Germany had been denied submarines until 1935, and the majority of the U-boats with which she went to war were of the *Type I* and *II* varieties, which were quickly relegated to training duties. There were, however, 18 *Type VII* and seven *Type IX* submarines; these were the forerunners of the most common types of U-boat built by Germany in the course of the war.

The Germans planned to use submarines in packs that could search for convoys and swamp the escort ships. Since, too, the intention was to use submarines in surface night attacks, the emphasis in their design was placed on torpedoes – not gunfire – and on speed and surface performance. Thus the *Type VII-B*, though only 753 tons, could make 17·25 knots on the surface (which was faster than a corvette of the *Flower* class). This class of submarine, which was virtually the same as Germany's most common type of submarine, the *Type VII-C*, had a 6,500-mile range and an armament of 12 torpedoes.

Another class of U-boat, the type *IX-A*, had a range of 8,100 miles, displaced 1,032 tons and carried 22 torpedoes. Subsequently the Germans developed the rather remarkable *Type IX-D2*, which, on a displacement of only 1,616 tons, carried 24 torpedoes and had a range of 23,700 miles at 12 knots; its maximum surface speed was 20 knots. However, only 30 of these craft were built.

German submarines proved satisfactory until the use of radar became widespread in British and American escorts. Until that time submarines enjoyed the advantage of near-invisibility during a night attack. But radar forced the Germans to resort to a vessel capable of operating and attacking from beneath the surface. The first solution to their problems was the snorkel, which had been developed by the Dutch Navy before the war. This was a breathing device that drew in fresh air and expelled fumes and so allowed the diesel engines to run when the submarine was submerged. The snorkel also provided greater security, since it was difficult for enemy radar to make contact with such a small and otherwise invisible target (though the 3-cm radar introduced in 1945 enjoyed reasonable success). However, the new security was achieved at the cost of mobility. Maximum speed fell to 6 knots, which was insufficient for concentration against a convoy or for escape from the escorts.

To solve this problem the Germans broke away from the accepted concept of the submarine – that of a surface craft that could dive. Priority was now given to underwater performance, which meant high submerged speeds and an improved battery capacity. These requirements produced the 1,621-ton *Type XXI* for ocean work, and the *Type XXIII* (232 tons) for coastal work. Whereas earlier submarines had a maximum submerged speed of eight knots for one hour, the *Type XXI* had a maximum speed of 17 knots for one hour – enough to out-run most escorts and their depth-charges. The new submarine could also make five knots on silent electrical motors for three days. But, for all their technical efficiency, only 123 *Type XXI*s and 59 *Type XXIII*s were completed before the end of the war; thus their appearance came far too late to affect the outcome.

Both the new types of submarine were considerable technical successes and major advances over earlier types. Also at this time the Germans were building a *Type XXVI*,

of which four were completed before the war. These were the Walther boats, whose high speed was obtained through a dangerous and expensive fuel, Ingolin, which was the energy source for a gas-driven, closed-circuit turbine. Exhausts dissolved in the sea and left no trace, while the closed circuit did not use up the submarine's air. The system gave high speed for long periods, but fuel consumption was high and the submarine needed diesel/electrical propulsion to reach the patrol areas. This meant that the submarine had three different sets of machinery. Its snorkelling performance, though poor, was offset by the development of improved hydrophones that enabled accurate salvoes of torpedoes to be fired at a depth of 150 feet.

Surface Actions

OPPOSITE *In the Mediterranean the Fleet Air Arm staged a successful raid on Taranto, sinking the battleship* Littorio *(left) and crippling two others. The aerial view shows the harbour after the attack.*
BELOW *The German pocket battleship* Graf Spee *in flames off Montevideo after the River Plate engagement that gave a lift to British morale in the first winter of the war.*

During World War II there were no major fleet actions in the European theatre. The Germans lacked a balanced fleet and usually sought to avoid action when opposed by units of the Royal Navy. Because of this, many convoys were saved from the attentions of German surface raiders.

Several engagements were fought out to a finish: the pocket battleship *Graf Spee* was hounded to an ignominious end by British cruisers in the River Plate in December 1939; the battleship *Bismarck*, crippled by air strikes as she made for Brest, was hammered into scrap by the guns of the Home Fleet, and the *Scharnhorst*, often a lucky ship, was sunk off the North Cape on 26 December 1943 in the last engagement in European waters between gunned capital ships. Only at Narvik, during the Norwegian campaign, did several actions take place. Most were fleeting and inconclusive, but at the Second Battle of Narvik the battleship *Warspite*, screened by nine destroyers, entered

the fjord and sank eight German destroyers. Revenge was extracted when Germany's two battlecruisers cornered and sank the aircraft carrier *Glorious* and her two destroyer escorts; this was the only action of the war in which a fleet carrier was sunk by gunned capital ships.

In the Mediterranean there was a similar lack of decisive action despite the presence of four fleets: the French, the Italian, and two British forces at Gibraltar and Alexandria. The first major action was Operation Catapult, the unfortunate attack on the French fleet at its anchorage at Oran. One battleship, the *Bretagne*, was sunk and two more crippled by the combined attentions of the *Hood*, *Valiant* and *Resolution*. Most of the actions in the Mediterranean were between aircraft, and submarines, against British surface units. In their efforts to keep Malta supplied, the British suffered very heavy losses, especially during Operation Pedestal in August 1942. Out of 14 merchant ships that set sail only four reached Malta, while one carrier was sunk and another crippled in their defence. Greece and Crete also cost the British heavy losses: at Crete three cruisers and six destroyers were lost and seven other ships, including two battleships and a carrier, were damaged beyond local repair. But losses were not all one way. A night attack by the Fleet Air Arm sunk one Italian

ABOVE *The war is over, and on her return from the Pacific theatre the US carrier* Enterprise *noses into the Miraflores locks on the Panama Canal, watched over by a Navy 'blimp'.*
LEFT *Gun turrets on board the US battleship* Arkansas.

battleship and crippled two more at Taranto; and three heavy cruisers and two destroyers were accounted for in a night action with the British battle fleet off Cape Matapan.

In the Pacific, fleet actions were more common, for in this theatre were two fleets that needed command of the seas and were prepared to fight for it. In an attempt to secure an overwhelming initial advantage, the Japanese attacked the US fleet at Pearl Harbor. Four American battleships were sunk in this pre-emptive attack (though two were subsequently recovered). Unfortunately for the Japanese, the oil installations, dockyard facilities and the carriers were not destroyed and Japan was forced to turn her attention to completing this task within six months of the outbreak of war. In the meantime, however, several battles had been fought. At the Battle of the Java Sea a mixed force of American, Dutch, British and Australian cruisers and destroyers was crushed, and on 9 April 1942 the British lost a carrier and two cruisers in the Indian Ocean to Japan's carrier aircraft. Between 4 and 8 May, however, the unbroken run of Japanese successes was halted at the

Battle of the Coral Sea. In this, the first naval battle to be fought entirely by aircraft, the Japanese lost the carrier *Shoho* and in return sank the *Lexington* and crippled the *Yorktown*. Thus although the balance of losses superficially favoured Japan, she could not in fact afford the loss of a single carrier at a time when American building was getting into its stride.

In an effort to bring about the destruction of the American carriers, the Japanese tried to make the Americans give battle by invading Midway Island. Aided by a knowledge of Japanese dispositions and intentions, the Americans fought a defensive battle which smashed Japan's main carrier force. Four Japanese carriers were sunk for the loss of the hastily-repaired *Yorktown*.

Midway ushered in a period of balance: neither side was powerful enough to seize the initiative and force its will upon the enemy. The Americans were strong enough, however, to contest Japanese activity in the Solomons. American landings on Guadalcanal on 7 August sparked off a series of actions which drained Japanese strength more severely than it depleted the US Navy. On 9 August one Australian and three American cruisers were sunk in the Battle of Savo Island as the Japanese sought to contest the landings. On 23–24 August, in the Battle of the Eastern Solomons, a Japanese attempt to supply its garrison resulted in the loss of the carrier *Ryuko* and, on the opposing side, the severe battering of the American carrier *Enterprise*. The fierce actions continued: Japanese submarines caused heavy damage to the carrier *Saratoga* on 31 August and sank the *Wasp* on 15 September. The Battle of Cape Esperance (11–12 October) was indecisive with losses approximately equal. The Battle of Santa Cruz,

fought two weeks later, saw the virtual elimination of the carrier forces of both sides. The Americans lost the *Hornet*, and the *Enterprise* was again badly mauled. In return the *Zuiho* and *Shokaku* were severely damaged. Thereafter it was the turn of the battleships. In a series of night actions between 12 and 15 November the Japanese lost two battleships, a cruiser and three destroyers in what turned out to be their last major effort at Guadalcanal. The American losses (two cruisers and eight destroyers) were a heavy price to pay but they could be accepted in view of American resources. In the last major action in these waters, the Japanese sank one cruiser and damaged three more at the Battle of Tassafaronga on 30 November. Japanese resistance on Guadalcanal ceased on 9 February 1943.

Thereafter the Americans were able to undertake an increasingly dynamic offensive. For most of 1943 action was mainly centred on the Solomons, as the Americans slowly drove up the island chain until in November the first landings were made in the Gilberts and Marshalls. The landings on Saipan the following June resulted in the Battle of the Philippine Sea, where the Japanese, giving battle for the first time for nearly two years, lost three carriers and over 400 aircraft in the last carrier battle of the war. The result of this battle effectively sealed the fate of Japan and her Navy. An attempt, in October, to counter the American landings at Leyte not only resulted in the last action between battleships (fought in the Surigao Strait) but in the annihilation of the Japanese fleet. Three battleships, four carriers, 10 cruisers and nine destroyers were sunk for the cost of one carrier, two escort carriers and three destroyers. From that point the Americans had little more to do than mop up the remainder.

BELOW *An aerial view of the Japanese heavy cruiser* Mikuma *burning during the Battle of Midway, June 1942. In this battle the Japanese lost four carriers.*

OPPOSITE, ABOVE *At the Battle of Cape Engano, 25 October 1944, the Japanese carrier* Zuiho *is attacked by aircraft from USS* Enterprise.

OPPOSITE, BELOW *Japanese planes attack and sink the USS* Hornet *at the Battle of Santa Cruz, 26 October 1942, in the face of scant anti-aircraft fire.*

BATTLE OF THE PHILIPPINE SEA, 18-21 JUNE 1944

The massive clashes in this battle between carrier-borne aircraft were characteristic of the new brand of long-range naval warfare. Thus Vice-Admiral Ozawa could plan a major assault on the US Fifth Fleet while keeping his own ships some 400 miles from the enemy's position until hours before the attack was launched. On the Allied side, Admiral Spruance knew that the outcome hinged on successfully exploiting his 2-1 superiority in naval aircraft.

The Airborne Forces
Spruance's deadly blend of 891 fighters, torpedo-bombers and dive-bombers eventually crushed the Japanese force of 430, of which barely 30 survived.

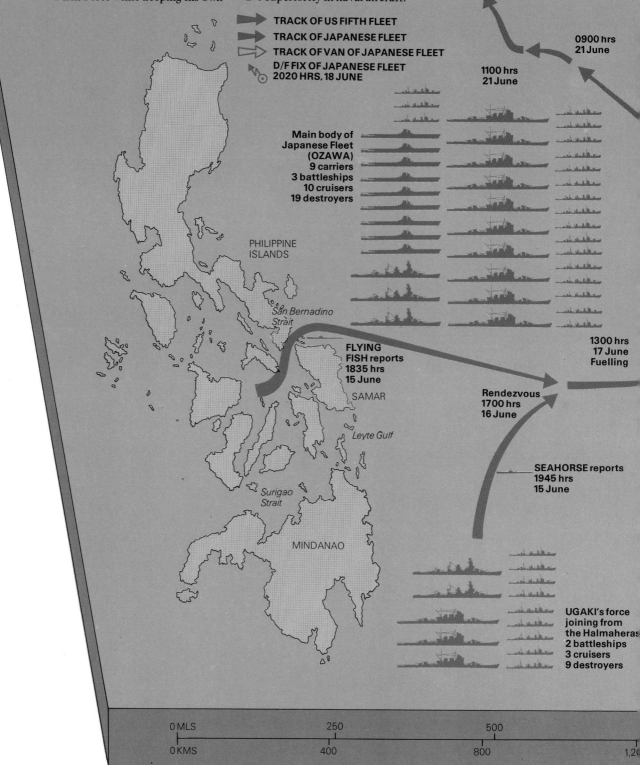

TRACK OF US FIFTH FLEET

TRACK OF JAPANESE FLEET

TRACK OF VAN OF JAPANESE FLEET

D/F FIX OF JAPANESE FLEET
2020 HRS, 18 JUNE

0900 hrs
21 June

1100 hrs
21 June

Main body of
Japanese Fleet
(OZAWA)
9 carriers
3 battleships
10 cruisers
19 destroyers

PHILIPPINE
ISLANDS

San Bernadino
Strait

FLYING
FISH reports
1835 hrs
15 June

SAMAR

1300 hrs
17 June
Fuelling

Rendezvous
1700 hrs
16 June

Leyte Gulf

SEAHORSE reports
1945 hrs
15 June

Surigao
Strait

MINDANAO

UGAKI's force
joining from
the Halmaheras
2 battleships
3 cruisers
9 destroyers

0 MLS   250   500

0 KMS   400   800   1,20

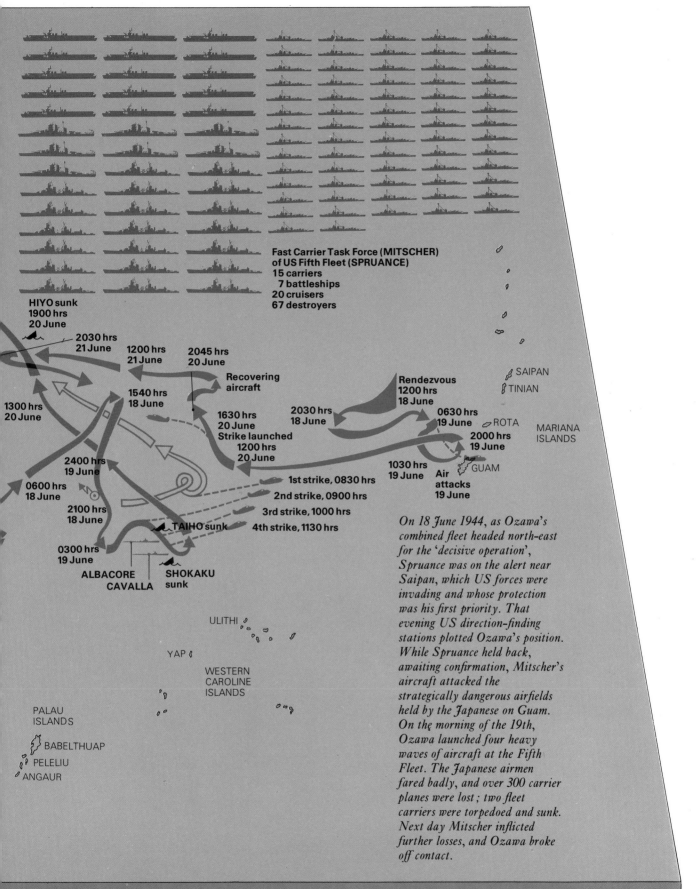

**Fast Carrier Task Force (MITSCHER)
of US Fifth Fleet (SPRUANCE)
15 carriers
7 battleships
20 cruisers
67 destroyers**

**HIYO sunk
1900 hrs
20 June**

**2030 hrs
21 June**

**1200 hrs
21 June**

**2045 hrs
20 June**

**Recovering
aircraft**

**1540 hrs
18 June**

**1300 hrs
20 June**

**1630 hrs
20 June
Strike launched
1200 hrs
20 June**

**2030 hrs
18 June**

**Rendezvous
1200 hrs
18 June**

**0630 hrs
19 June**

**2000 hrs
19 June**

**2400 hrs
19 June**

**0600 hrs
18 June**

**2100 hrs
18 June**

**1030 hrs
19 June**

**Air
attacks
19 June**

1st strike, 0830 hrs

2nd strike, 0900 hrs

3rd strike, 1000 hrs

4th strike, 1130 hrs

**0300 hrs
19 June**

TAIHO sunk

**ALBACORE
CAVALLA**

**SHOKAKU
sunk**

SAIPAN
TINIAN

ROTA

MARIANA
ISLANDS

GUAM

ULITHI

YAP

WESTERN
CAROLINE
ISLANDS

PALAU
ISLANDS

BABELTHUAP

PELELIU

ANGAUR

*On 18 June 1944, as Ozawa's
combined fleet headed north-east
for the 'decisive operation',
Spruance was on the alert near
Saipan, which US forces were
invading and whose protection
was his first priority. That
evening US direction-finding
stations plotted Ozawa's position.
While Spruance held back,
awaiting confirmation, Mitscher's
aircraft attacked the
strategically dangerous airfields
held by the Japanese on Guam.
On the morning of the 19th,
Ozawa launched four heavy
waves of aircraft at the Fifth
Fleet. The Japanese airmen
fared badly, and over 300 carrier
planes were lost; two fleet
carriers were torpedoed and sunk.
Next day Mitscher inflicted
further losses, and Ozawa broke
off contact.*

1,000	1,250	1,500	1,750
1,600	2,000	2,400	2,800

An American destroyer speeds into action as, in the background, the USS Intrepid lists heavily after being hit by a Japanese suicide plane; this photograph was taken from the USS Alaska.

INSET An American LCT-5 (Landing Craft Tank) on manoeuvres in Chesapeake Bay in 1943.

Chapter Seven
The Age of Deterrents

At the end of World War II there were, in effect, only two navies – those of the United States and Great Britain and her Empire. The navies of their enemies had, for the most part, ceased to exist and those of other nations were of little account. The Soviet Navy was quite strong on paper, for it disposed of one battleship, a couple of cruisers, some 20 destroyers and over 100 submarines. But in fact it was very weak. Its performance during the war had not been impressive, its training was of a low standard and its equipment obsolescent. Much of its manpower had been lost in the course of the land fighting on the Eastern Front. Added to this was the fact that the fleet had to be divided among all the seas that wash the Soviet Union.

The US Navy emerged from the war as the world's largest naval force. The Royal Navy was dwarfed in comparison yet it it was the only navy that could be realistically assessed against the American fleets. With over 3,600 named vessels, of which 23 were battleships, 20 were fleet carriers, eight were light carriers and 71 were escort carriers, the US Navy was more powerful than all the other navies of the world combined. In addition to this already overwhelming strength, American yards were building a further 21 carriers, all but two of which were fleet carriers. US naval aviation boasted 40,000 aircraft with more than 60,000 qualified pilots. By comparison, the Royal Navy possessed seven fleet carriers, five light carriers, 38 escort carriers and over 1,300 aircraft – still an extremely powerful force but one that now had to face the harsh realities of peacetime. One unpalatable truth was that an impoverished Britain, committed to a much-needed programme of post-war reform and reconstruction, could no longer afford to build and maintain a powerful fleet. Another arose from the simple fact that 34 escort carriers and over two-thirds of the aircraft – including most of the high-performance aircraft – had been supplied by and had to be returned to the United States.

Immediately after the war the American and the British fleets entered a period of decline. The immediate reduction of government spending was bound to affect the Navies and for a time new construction was halted and ships were

OPPOSITE *A salvo from the 16-inch guns of the USS* Missouri, *in action at Chong Jin, Korea.*
BELOW *After the Bomb – the USS* New York *is hosed down after the second atomic bomb test at Bikini, September 1946. This was done to wash away radio-active material before an inspection party was sent aboard to test how the ship had withstood the blast.*

A demonstration of US carrier power.

LEFT *The USS* Forrestal *on manoeuvres with the Sixth Fleet. The broad white line running diagonally across the flight deck is used by the pilots of landing aircraft to correct their line of approach. Both take-offs and landings can be handled simultaneously from the* Forrestal's *massive flight deck.*

TOP *Crew members of the* Forrestal *standing on the deck-edge elevator are transferring a Navy Skyhawk jet from the hangar to the flight deck prior to launching.*

ABOVE *The US nuclear fleet during Operation Sea Orbit. The ships are the carrier* Enterprise, *the* Long Beach *and the* Bainbridge.

Seen here is a cutaway of the USS George Washington (1959) the first submarine to fire a missile from beneath the surface of the sea.

1 Engine room
2 Reactor room
3 Missile room
4 Missile control centre
5 Navigation room
6 Gyro room
7 Stores
8 Batteries
9 Bridge
10 Periscope room
11 Control room
12 Crew's quarters
13 Crew's mess
14 Officers' wardroom
15 Forward torpedo room

OPPOSITE *A Polaris missile breaks the ocean surface after being fired from the submerged HMS* Revenge.

BELOW RIGHT *HMS* Revenge, *seen on exercise in 1970.*

RIGHT *The launching of the* George Washington, *which in 1960 became the first submarine to fire a missile from beneath the surface of the sea. At that period she was armed with 16 Polaris missiles: these had a single warhead and range of 1,500 miles. Since then the Poseidon missile has entered service: each of these contains ten 50-kiloton warheads. Accuracy has been improved and range increased to 2,875 miles.*

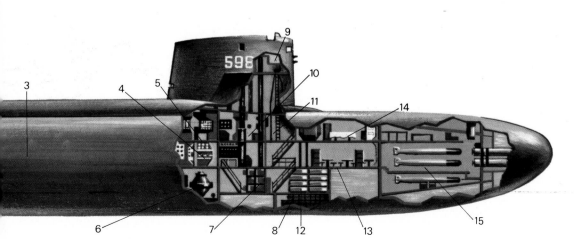

paid off. Neither the onset of the Cold War nor the build-up of the Soviet Navy redeemed the fortunes of the Western navies, for at the time there was no real naval threat from the Soviet Union. The US Navy also failed to secure for itself a nuclear role. It wanted to have nuclear weapons for its carriers, but it lost its case to the newly-formed US Air Force, which in the B-36 had an effective long-range bomber that could penetrate Soviet air space. After the war, with no other nation possessing the atomic bomb and the United States in possession of a massive strategic bombing force, there was no real need for the Americans to have several different means of delivering the deterrent. It is therefore hardly surprising that the US Navy failed to win the argument. Later, by 1950, the US Navy had been reduced in strength to seven fleet carriers.

The outbreak of the Korean War in 1950 restored the fortunes of the US Navy. The need for naval strength in helping to fight 'limited wars' and the great flexibility bestowed by carriers were clearly shown. By the end of the war the US Navy had 18 carriers in commission of which 11 saw action. The air strength they provided was extremely important in securing air supremacy, supporting land operations and maintaining a blockade of the North Korean coast. Battleships and cruisers, fitted with radar-controlled guns, also played a vital part in giving gun support and covering invasions and evacuations. The possibility of further Koreas ensured that after the war the US Navy would not have her conventional forces run down as they had been after 1945. On the other hand, by 1953 the Soviet Union had obtained a thermo-nuclear capability and was improving her air defences. The Americans now saw, despite the impending arrival of the highly advanced B-52 bomber to replace the B-36, that there was a need for more delivery systems. Thus the

OPPOSITE *The first launching of a Polaris missile from a surfaced vessel, the US nuclear-powered submarine* Henry Clay. *The debris is from the launch adaptors, which automatically detach themselves on launching. The slight list of the submarine is intentional, being a standard part of surfaced launch procedure.*

TOP *A Russian submarine during a naval parade; she is equipped to fire underwater-to-surface and surface-to-surface missiles.*

CENTRE *A J class Russian submarine.*

LEFT *Rendezvous at sea between a Soviet helicopter and a submarine.*

US Navy was ensured a nuclear role through its carriers and its new submarines.

The new carriers that were built owed much to British development, for the Royal Navy was not deficient in technique, only in numbers. In 1952 trials were conducted with an angled flight-deck on HMS *Triumph*. This arrangement allowed the storage of aircraft on the flight-deck and the landing and dispatching of aircraft to be conducted at the same time; this had been impossible with the ordinary flight-deck because of the danger of a landing aircraft overshooting. At the same time, too, the standard hydro-pneumatic catapults were replaced by more powerful steam versions, and flight-deck mirrors were incorporated to aid landings (a system first proposed by the Japanese in the 1920s). These British-developed features were worked into USS *Forrestal*, which Congress authorized in 1951. This ship, displacing over 60,000 tons, was the first American ship too large to use the Panama Canal. The longer landings and take-offs needed by jets, as compared to earlier aircraft, meant that she was over 1,000 feet long; her maximum beam, 152 feet, incorporated deck-edge lifts and an overhanging bridge.

The *Forrestal* was followed by the *Enterprise*, the first, and to date the only nuclear-powered carrier in commission. Research and development costs incurred during her construction left the American taxpayer with a bill for $451,000,000; and the increasing costs of reactors, materials and labour mean that the nuclear carriers being built in the USA at the present time will cost much more. The *Nimitz* (CVAN-68) will cost about $540,000,000 and

OPPOSITE *A Soviet-built Egyptian submarine of the W class.*
BELOW *The scene on the flight deck of the commando carrier HMS Albion. Helicopters have a growing role to play as reconnaissance machines and as interceptors armed with air-to-ship missiles. With the advent of more sophisticated 'listening' devices, the helicopter is also an effective submarine hunter/killer.*

the *Eisenhower* (CVAN-69) about $510,000,000; the unnamed CVAN-70, due to be started in 1974, is likely to cost more than $1,000,000,000 and her aircraft more than the *Nimitz* herself.

The *Enterprise* has proved a considerable technical and operational success. The lack of a funnel eliminated corrosion and turbulence whilst her unique power source gives her immense flexibility and virtually unlimited high-speed endurance. On her original uranium cores she steamed more than 200,000 miles; on one cruise, Exercise Sea Orbit, she steamed 30,565 miles in 65 days without resupply of any kind. She made five Vietnam tours; during one tour, in December 1965, a record number of air strikes in a single day (165) flew from her decks. Her immunity from attack contrasted strongly with the vulnerability of aircraft in bases in the south to Vietcong and North Vietnamese Army rocket attack.

Nuclear power was incorporated into American submarines slightly before it was used in the *Enterprise*. It was used not in the weapons but in the power source; thus the first application of nuclear power was aimed at improving the submarine's performance (rather than changing its role). The result was more or less the true submarine – a craft designed to operate completely submerged for an indefinite period. The first nuclear submarine, USS *Nautilus*, was commissioned in January 1955. Displacing 3,180 tons, she had a submerged speed of 20 knots and auxiliary electric motors. She was armed with conventional torpedoes but the following year the first submarine designed to carry nuclear missiles, the *Halibut*, was laid down. She was equipped with three Regulus missiles that could be fired only when the submarine was surfaced. This weakness was remedied in July 1960 when the *George Washington*, which was armed with 16 Polaris missiles, became the first submarine to fire a missile from beneath the surface of the sea.

The early Polaris missiles carried a single warhead and had a 1,500-mile range; since then both power and range have been increased. In 1964 the UGM-27C missile was first deployed. This missile carried a single 1-megaton warhead over 2,800 miles; subsequently the payload was converted into three smaller warheads. In 1971 the Poseidon UGM-73A missile entered service. This missile has a MIRV[1] capability with ten 50 kiloton warheads per missile – an arrangement that, combined with improvements in target accuracy, makes the Poseidon submarine many times more powerful than the Polaris craft. The US Navy has programmes for 31 Poseidon-carrying submarines with a total of 4,960 warheads.

After World War II the Soviet Union built up a numerically powerful fleet. The emphasis was placed on submarines and coastal craft to protect the flanks of the Red Army

[1] The abbreviation MIRV stands for multiple independently-targetable re-entry vehicle(s).

OPPOSITE *An aerial view of the flight deck of HMS* Ark Royal.
TOP *Trials in 1970 of the British Harrier V/Stol (Vertical take-off and landing) aircraft.*
ABOVE *Wessex and Sioux helicopters overfly HMS* Bulwark *as she refuels from the* Derwentdale.
BELOW *An artist's impression of the Royal Navy's latest ship type, the Through Deck Cruiser; she will act as a small-scale carrier, equipped with Sea King helicopters and a version of the Harrier.*

and to counter any Western amphibious attack. (The fleet's independent long-range capacity was limited – just a few cruisers, designed for commerce-raiding.) Soviet submarine strength probably rose to a peak of about 400; from that point Soviet policy seems to have concentrated on replacing older types by new, long-range submarines.

The development of a nuclear-powered submarine armed with nuclear missiles gave the Soviet Union the opportunity to possess for the first time a credible deterrent against the United States. Whereas the Americans saw the submarine as an alternative delivery system to their aircraft and land-based missiles, the Soviets in the late 1950s and early '60s saw the submarine as *the* means of delivery, for at that time they lacked long-range bombers and their missiles could only be effective against Western Europe.

The submarine, by carrying the short-ranged missiles to within range of the American coasts, provided the first means of striking at the United States homeland. Since 1958 the Soviets have deployed submarines carrying nuclear weapons, but initially these were conventional diesel craft that had to surface to fire their few, short-ranged missiles. These *G* and *H* class submarines, 24 of which are still operational, carried the SSN-4 Sark and SSN-5 Serb missiles in threes. During the 1960s the Soviets developed the SSN-6 Sawfly missile, which had a 1-megaton warhead and a 1,750-mile range; they also built nuclear-powered submarines which, like their American counterparts, carry 16 missiles.

Thus the two super-powers have built up through their nuclear submarines powerful deterrents that are reasonably cheap, extremely flexible and, for the moment, invulnerable. The importance of the submarine has increased and the power of the bomber, even when equipped with stand-off weapons, has declined as air-defence systems have improved. Up to the present time the submarine has been able to keep ahead of anti-submarine techniques; moreover, submarines and missiles of greatly improved capability are being developed. This is being done partly through fear that some anti-submarine breakthrough may also be achieved in the near future, and partly as a means of trying to keep ahead of the enemy, if only to provide diplomatic 'chips' for future arms limitation talks.

At the moment only small parts of the world's oceans are suited to a nuclear submarine on patrol, for the submarine is limited by the range of its missiles and the depth to which it can dive. It is possible, too, that detection could reach a point at which submarines could be tracked through such measures as sonar positioned on the seabed or dipped from surface craft. For the time being this seems either unlikely or at least a long-term prospect. However, deeper-diving submarines armed with longer-ranged missiles would make the task of tracking much harder. In response to this notion the Soviet Union has developed new missiles with ranges of up to 3,500 miles, which will be carried in the latest *Y* class submarine. The US Navy's plans include a new submarine and new missiles. The new missile is the Trident-1 (C-4) which is a

Submarine weaponry
The diagram illustrates, in ideal form, how versatile submarines could become in the near future. The operational system shown here was devised by Vickers Ltd, and revolves around the SLAM (Submarine Launched Airflight Missile); a photograph of the missile system is at far right. The six Blowpipe missiles have a range of two miles.

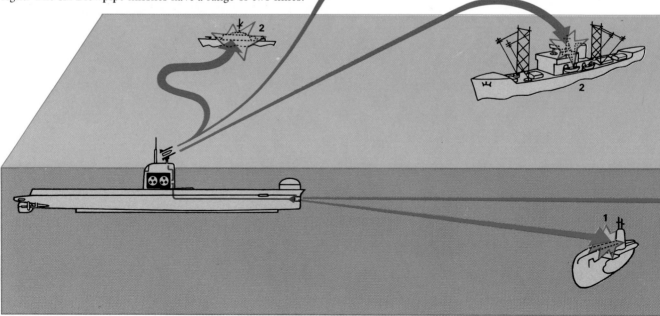

At the heart of this submarine is a computerized data system that displays the tactical picture to the onboard command. Decisions can then be taken whether or not to fire:
1 *Anti-ship or anti-submarine torpedoes.*
2 *Blowpipe missiles from the SLAM system, for short-range use against hostile ships or helicopters.*
3 *USGWs, for use against enemy warships.*

ABOVE *The American guided missile cruiser* Albany *fires three surface-to-air test missiles simultaneously from forward, aft and one side of the ship.*

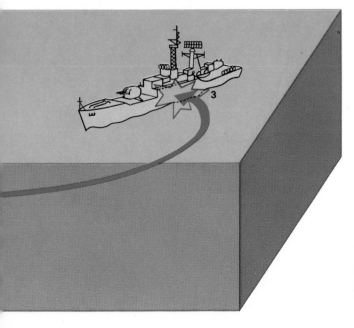

boosted Poseidon with a 4,350-mile range; this should be deployed in 1978. The subsequent Trident-2 is to have a 6,000-mile range. From their base at Bangor, Washington State, submarines carrying this missile would be within range of any worthwhile target anywhere in China and the USSR without even leaving harbour. The submarines would displace at least 12,000 tons and would carry a minimum of 20, perhaps as many as 24 missiles. The cost per submarine would be in the region of $1,300,000,000 – a price that seems excessive in the light of America's present overkill capability.

This weapon, which has a half-hour range at 50 knots, is designed for action against either surface or submerged craft. Its maximum depth is 3,000 feet and it can be wire-guided until its own homing device picks up its target. Finally, there is the Submarine Launched Airflight Missile (SLAM), which is being developed by the Royal Navy; trials were carried out in 1972. The system features an armament of six Blowpipe missiles built around a camera and infra-red sensor. The Blowpipe, which is a thumb-operated, one-man anti-aircraft missile originally built for land forces, has a range of two miles and a five-pound

ABOVE *The British destroyer HMS* Devonshire *fires a Sea Slug missile on trials off the Scottish coast. The Sea Slug is 20 feet long and can be used against both surface and air targets.*
RIGHT *Shown here is the Sea Cat missile on demonstration in the Baltic with the Swedish ship* Sodermanland. *The British-built Sea Cat is in service with more than a dozen navies; it has a range of 2·2 miles. In an anti-aircraft role these missiles can be deployed in seconds against low flying fighters.*

It is hardly surprising that, with so much emphasis and money placed on the nuclear submarine and its missiles, the conventional submarine and its armament should to some extent have been neglected. That the latter have become the Cinderellas of their fleets is demonstrated, for example, by the fact that the Royal Navy's submarines are still equipped with a torpedo designed before 1939. But in the last few years developments have considerably increased the power of the conventional submarine. Possibly the most important, certainly the most spectacular of these is the Under Surface Guided Weapon (USGW). This weapon will allow the submarine to attack a searching enemy warship beyond the increasing range of anti-submarine weapon systems. Able to operate from 21-inch torpedo tubes, the USGW breaks the surface and, travelling through the air, homes on the enemy ship. It may also be possible for future USGWs to re-enter the water to attack a submarine.

Another major development is the M-48 torpedo that entered service with the US Navy in February 1972.

warhead. Such a weapon could be extremely useful in counter-attacking an enemy helicopter.

The increasing sophistication of weapons and the growing cost of ships has led in the last ten years to the navies of the lesser powers being all but priced out of existence. In the present climate of rising costs and increasing complexity, only the Soviet Union and the United States can afford new weapon systems – and even these nations are beginning to feel the strain. At the present moment the US Navy still retains a considerable superiority over the Soviet Navy. The former can always have more nuclear submarines on station at any one time and can use them to better effect than the Soviets, who lack overseas bases and are still handicapped by their long tail of old submarines and missiles. Moreover, American carrier strength, usually decried by the Soviets as obsolescent, gives the West an overwhelming advantage over the Soviets, who lack an integrated naval air defence.

To try to offset American air supremacy, the Soviets are working on their first carriers. No details have been announced but space surveillance suggests that the first will be about 40,000 tons and over 900 feet long. Although she will have an angled flight-deck, it seems unlikely that she will carry either catapults or a full-length flight-

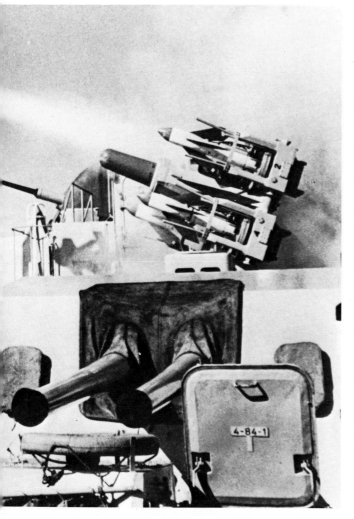

deck; the forecastle will carry missiles and AA guns. It seems probable that she will be equipped with fixed-wing aircraft – but she could conceivably be a commando carrier, equipped to carry amphibious troops.

The building of a carrier by the USSR has coincided with the decline of the carrier in the British Navy. Rising costs and the increasing problem of manning the fleet since the abolition of national service have resulted in the passing of all the fleet carriers but one. She, the *Ark Royal*, was also to have been phased out by 1972, but a change of government brought about a stay of execution. That the Royal Navy has only one carrier means that there are periods when Britain has no carrier at sea at all. The *Ark Royal* also has several major counts against her. Despite her 50,000 tons she carries relatively few aircraft – only 36. And her many refits and facelifts have failed to disguise the fact that she is really of World War II vintage and cannot keep going forever.

To replace her the Royal Navy has ordered HMS *Invincible*, the first of what should be a new type of ship, the Through Deck Cruiser. This ship is designed to be a command and control unit as much as a ship that can give an integrated recce, strike and air-defence capability. In essence the cruisers will be mini-carriers that displace about 20,000 tons. Sea Dart missiles will provide a surface-to-surface and a surface-to-air capability with Sea King helicopters, equipped with their own sonar and weapons, acting in an anti-submarine role. It is believed, indeed there would be little point in building such ships unless it were so, that the Through Deck Carrier will carry a version of the Harrier V/STOL (Vertical/short take-off and landing). The ship, 630 feet long, should have a top speed of about 30 knots with gas turbines and would cost about £30,000,000. Obviously more than one needs to be built if such ships are to play any important role in the fleet.

The reliance of the Western navies upon the aircraft for attack purposes, combined with the high cost of ships and armaments, has led over the last 20 years to specialization on the part of the smaller ships. Ships have tended to concentrate primarily on either an ASW or an AA role, almost to the exclusion of the other capability. The reasons for the parallel decline in big ships that could combine both systems are largely related to their high cost both in terms of money and skilled manpower.

It seems likely that in future ships will have to carry, either internally or through a helicopter, an anti-ship weapons system. In 1967 the Israeli destroyer *Eilat* was sunk by a Soviet-built fast patrol boat that never left harbour. The heavily gunned destroyer, taken by surprise, was sunk by SSN-2 Styx missiles. This event intensified a search for equivalent weapons in the Western navies. At the moment Norway, Sweden, Israel and the United States have ship-to-ship missiles in service whilst the French are developing the Exocet missile by themselves and the Otomat missile in conjunction with the Italians. The latter has a 40-mile range and will need a relay if it is to be used to its full potential, i.e. against targets beyond the horizon line.

The helicopter offers a means of intercepting an attacking patrol boat before it closes to decisive range. The Royal Navy has developed the CI-834 missile for use in the Anglo–French Lynx helicopter in order to achieve this. The Italians have also developed an air-to-ship missile, the Airtos. This weapon has a 7-mile range at a speed of up to Mach 2; target acquisition – the point at which the weapon sees and locks on to a target – is at 10 miles. The weapon is supposed to be effective against targets moving at speeds of up to 90 knots – a performance that will probably be needed if interceptions are to be made against future hydrofoils and fast patrol boats.

The British have several missiles with a ship-to-ship capability but, for the most part, these weapons are primarily ship-to-air missiles. In the late 1950s the Sea Cat missile was developed and has since seen service in more than a dozen navies. Like the new French missile, the Roland, it is a close-range weapon. The Sea Slug and the Sea Dart followed the Sea Cat into service, but the Royal Navy's next missile, the Sea Wolf, has run into major cost and development difficulties, for it is already late and will cost at least twice the original estimate. It is designed to give an improved defence against aircraft and missiles travelling at Mach 2. The Italians have, for their anti-aircraft protection, modifications of either the Indigo or the Albatros missiles. The Indigo was originally land-based and has a ceiling of 6,000 metres and a slant range of 6·25 miles. The Albatros uses air-to-air missiles against missiles and aircraft.

The rapid development of missiles has not, to date, led to the suppression of the gun. Indeed, the majority of ships in service still retain guns and it is likely that this situation will persist for some time. The gun still has several very important advantages over the missile, not least its cheapness. In addition, its robustness, its high rate of fire and its ability to engage air, sea and land targets at horizon range (approx. 16 miles) still make it an extremely attractive weapon. The largest naval guns are the nine 16-inch guns of the battleship *New Jersey*, which were used in coastal operations off South Vietnam (the cost of recommissioning this ship for active service was approximately $21,000,000). The latest French gun, the 100-mm, is fully automatic and can fire 60 rounds a minute. Smaller anti-aircraft weapons are used for close-range defence.

The shift in the balance between missile and gun since the end of World War II has been matched by a shift in the overall balance of power, the most obvious features of which have been the relative decline of the European powers and the emergence of the Soviet Navy as an oceanic force capable of securing local command of the sea and also of contesting the West's general superiority. Nevertheless, even without the United States NATO outnumbers those naval forces that the Soviets could deploy against it, while the level of serviceability maintained by the European powers is generally higher than that of the Soviets and Americans.

The West's margin of naval superiority, so overwhelming in 1945, remains undisputed in one vital respect – the integrated air arm of the US Navy; and this is likely to remain the case for some time. In other fields the Soviet challenge has been more strongly made; the results of this can clearly be seen in our concluding table.

BELOW *A Russian Fast Patrol Boat. These compact vessels are used to deliver anti-ship missiles of the SSN-2 Styx type. In the West a number of parallel developments in the missile field are taking place, including the Exocet missile which the French are building and the Italian Otomat, which has a range of 40 miles.*

The Balance of Naval Power 1973—74

Although the seven nations listed differ in the way they interpret the functions of their ships, most of the major differences are accounted for in the footnotes. In addition, American strengths do not include the US Marine Corps, while Soviet figures include the Naval Air Force and Naval Infantry. Air strengths, where appropriate, embrace all types of aircraft, including helicopters. The US Navy's reserve strength is given in parentheses.

The high Soviet and Chinese totals for coastal defence craft, etc., and landing ships and craft are reached partly through including ships of small size not incorporated in Western naval lists. China has one submarine with missile tubes, but it is not known whether it has any missiles. The US Navy possesses many more mine warfare ships than the 92 major units indicated.

CATEGORY	USA	USSR	GB	FRANCE	CHINA	S VIETNAM	JAPAN
Manpower in 000s	564 (131)	475	81	69	180	45	41
Surface ships in commission	221 (54)	212	78	47	n/a	n/a	n/a
Nuclear submarines of all types	60	65	8	4	1 (?)	—	—
Other submarines	24 (8)	220	22	19	48	—	13
Aircraft (S=squadrons, AT=all types, CA=combat aircraft)	163 (70)S	1,160AT	17S	15S	n/a	n/a	110CA
Battleships	(4)	—	—	—	—	—	—
Attack aircraft carriers	15 (6)	—	1	2	—	—	—
Other aircraft carriers	—	—	2	1[g]	—	—	—
SAM cruisers	8 (2)	—	2	2[h]	—	—	—
Other types of cruiser	1 (12)	32[a]	—	—	—	—	—
SAM frigates	28	—	—	—	—	—	—
Other types of frigates	(2)	—	62[f]	25	—	9	—
SAM destroyers	29	32[b]	9	6	—	—	1
Other types of destroyer	71 (43)	44[c]	—	11	6[i]	—	28
SAM destroyer-escorts	6	—	—	—	—	—	—
Other destroyer escorts	62 (33)	269[d]	—	—	9	—	14
Amphibious warfare ships inc. landing ships and craft	65 (74)	233	2	20	570[j]	40	53
Various types of mine warfare craft	10 (82)	295	44	46	72	2	45
Logistics and operations support craft	150 (75)	n/a	56	12	n/a	n/a	n/a
Coastal defence, Fast Patrol Boats and torpedo boats	n/a	327[e]	11	14	596	55	5
Riverine craft	—	—	—	—	—	800	—
Diesel junks	—	—	—	—	—	250	—

Australia, India, Argentina and Brazil are the only other nations to have aircraft carriers, that of Brazil being ASW. All are ex-British Navy carriers (that of Argentina reaching her via the Royal Netherlands Navy), and are of less than 20,000 tons fully laden with no more than 20 aircraft. Like the British carriers listed, all were laid down during World War II and must now be approaching the end of their active lives.

[a] Of which 2 ASW helicopter, 14 gunned and 16 with SSM and SAM capabilities. [b] Four have SSM also. [c] Of which 7 have SSM. [d] Oceanic and coastal. [e] Of which 187 carry Styx SSM. [f] Of which 20 ASW. [g] Helicopter carrier. [h] Including 1 helicopter cruiser. [i] All SSM. [j] Of which 25 carry Styx SSM.

Key to Abbreviations

SAM	Surface-to-air missiles
ASW	Anti-submarine warfare
SSM	Surface-to-surface missiles

DATA SECTION
1: Significant Warships 1860-1970
2: Missiles of the World's Navies

Except where stated otherwise, the date for each ship refers to the year it was laid down; length is measured between perpendiculars, i.e. between the rudder post and the bow end of the main deck; displacement figures represent standard displacement.

Armoured Frigate WARRIOR

(Britain) 1860

Displacement	9,210 tons
Length	380 feet
Beam	58 feet 6 inches
Draught	26 feet
Armament (first)	26 × 68 pounder muzzle-loaders
	14 × 110 pounder breech-loaders
	4 × 70 pounder breech-loaders
Main armour	4·5 inch belt
Engines	5,500 hp; trunk
Speed	14 knots (steam)
	10 knots (sail)

The world's first iron ship; subsequently re-armed solely with 68-pounders.

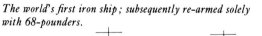
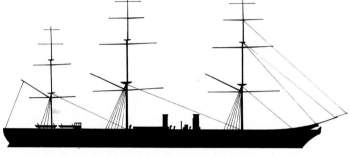

Armoured turretship MONARCH

(Britain) 1868

Displacement	8,300 tons
Length	330 feet
Beam	57 feet
Draught	26 feet
Armament (first)	4 × 12 inch rifled muzzle-loaders
	3 × 7 inch rifled muzzle-loaders
Main armour	7·5 to 4·5 inch sides
	4·5 inch bulkheads
	10 to 8 inch turrets
Engines	7,840 hp; return connecting-rod
Speed	14 knots (steam)
	13 knots (sail)

The first ocean-going ship equipped with turrets (2), which carried the main armament.

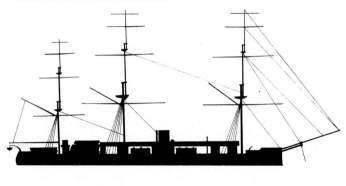

Battleship DUILIO

(Italy) 1872

Displacement	11,200 tons
Length	340 feet
Beam	64 feet
Draught	26 feet 9 inches
Armament	4 × 17·7 inch guns
	4 × 10 inch guns
	7 × 6·1 inch guns
	5 × 4·7 inch guns
	16 × 57 mm guns
	2 × 37 mm guns
Max. armour	22 inches (sides)
Engines	7,700 hp
Speed	11 knots

A world-leader in the race to produce a monster-gunned battleship.

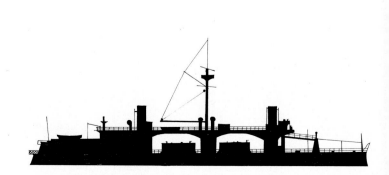

Battleship MAJESTIC

(Britain) 1893

Class	Majestic
Displacement	14,900 tons
Length	390 feet
Beam	75 feet
Draught	26 feet 6 inches
Armament	4 × 12 inch guns
	12 × 6 inch guns
	16 × 12 pounders
	12 × 3 pounders
	5 × 18 inch torpedo tubes (1 stern mounted, 4 submerged)
Main armour	9 inch belt
Engines	10,000 hp; triple expansion
Speed	16 knots

First of a new class of battleship using Harvey steel armour (which allowed a 50% reduction in thickness for the same protection) and the new wire-wound 12-inch gun.

Battleship KENTUCKY

(USA) 1896

Class	Kearsarge (2 built)
Displacement	11,540 tons
Length	375 feet 4 inches
Beam	72 feet 3 inches
Draught	23 feet 6 inches
Armament	4 × 13 inch guns
	4 × 8 inch guns
	14 × 5 inch guns
	20 × 6 pounder guns
	4 × 18 inch torpedo tubes
Main armour	17 to 9 inch belt
Engines	10,000 hp; reciprocating
Speed	16 knots

US battleship featuring three gun-types in the main armament (13-inch, 8-inch and 5-inch).

Battleship KING EDWARD VII

(Britain) 1903

Class	King Edward VII (8 built)
Displacement	16,350 tons
Length	453 feet 9 inches
Beam	78 feet
Draught	25 feet
Armament	4 × 12 inch guns
	4 × 9·2 inch guns
	10 × 6 inch guns
	14 × 12 pounders
	14 × 3 pounders
	4 × 18 inch torpedo tubes
Main armour	9 to 4 inch belt
Engines	18,000 hp; triple expansion
Speed	18·5 knots

One of a new class of more heavily armed British battleships built to keep pace with developments overseas.

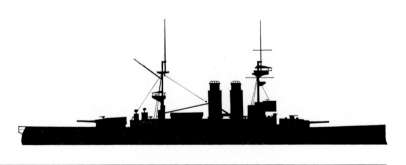

Battleship DREADNOUGHT

(Britain) 1906

Class	Dreadnought
Displacement	17,900 tons
Length	527 feet
Beam	82 feet
Draught	26 feet 6 inches
Armament	10 × 12 inch guns
	27 × 12 pounders
	5 × 18 inch torpedo tubes
Main armour	11 to 4 inch belt
Engines	23,000 hp; turbines
Speed	21 knots

A revolutionary design centred round a uniform heavy armament; the name became a universal description for ships of her type.

Battleship SOUTH CAROLINA

(USA) 1906

Class	South Carolina (2 built)
Displacement	16,000 tons
Length	452 feet 9 inches
Beam	80 feet 3 inches
Draught	24 feet 6 inches
Armament	8 × 12 inch guns
	22 × 3 inch guns
	2 × 21 inch torpedo tubes
Main armour	12 to 9 inch belt
Engines	16,500 hp; reciprocating
Speed	18·5 knots

One of the first American dreadnoughts; her superimposed gun arrangement was a major design innovation later adopted by all nations.

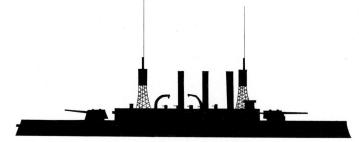

Battleship FUSO

(Japan) 1912

Displacement	29,330 tons
Length	630 feet
Beam	94 feet
Draught	28 feet 4 inches
Armament	12 × 14 inch guns
	16 × 6 inch guns
	4 × 3 inch AA guns
	6 × 21 inch torpedo tubes
Main armour	12 to 4 inch belt
Engines	40,000 hp; turbines
Speed	23 knots

With this ship the Japanese increased the heavy armament of their dreadnoughts to 14-inch guns.

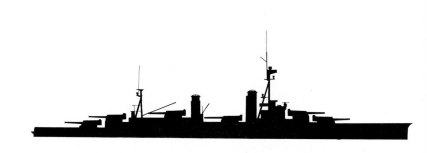

Battlecruiser INVINCIBLE

(Britain) 1907

Class	Invincible (3 built)
Displacement	17,250 tons
Length	567 feet
Beam	78 feet 6 inches
Draught	25 feet 6 inches
Armament	8 × 12 inch guns
	16 × 4 inch guns
	1 × 3 inch gun
	5 × 18 inch torpedo tubes
Main armour	6 to 4 inch belt
Engines	41,000 hp; turbines
Speed	28 knots

First of a new type of warship designed to act independently in fast battle-squadrons and to scout for and support the battleships.

Battlecruiser VON DER TANN

(Germany) 1907

Displacement	21,000 tons
Length	561 feet (overall)
Beam	85 feet
Draught	27 feet
Armament	8 × 11 inch guns
	10 × 6 inch guns
	16 × 24 pounder guns
	4 × 18 inch torpedo tubes
Main armour	9·75 to 7 inch belt
Engines	50,000 hp; turbines
Speed	25 knots

Germany's first battlecruiser, better equipped defensively than her British rivals.

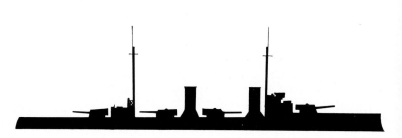

Torpedo-boat destroyers TRIBAL
(Britain) 1906–8

Class	Tribal (12 built)
Displacement	850 to 1,045 tons
Length	250 to 280 feet
Beam	25 to 27 feet
Draught	15 to 17 feet
Armament (first)	3 × 12 pounders
	2 × 18 inch torpedo tubes
Engines	21,000 to 27,000 hp; turbines
Speed	33 knots

First class of British destroyers to have turbines; also first to burn oil in place of coal. Later ships of this class were armed with two 4-inch 25-pounder guns.

Cruiser IRIS
(Britain) 1878

Displacement	3,730 tons
Length	331 feet 6 inches
Beam	46 feet
Draught	22 feet
Armament (first)	10 × 64 pounder muzzle-loaders
	4 torpedo tubes
Engines	6,000 hp; compound
Speed	18·6 knots

This fast ship (still equipped with auxiliary sail to save coal stocks) was the first steel cruiser; she was designed to scout for the battle fleet and to protect and prey on commercial shipping.

Torpedo boat LIGHTNING
(Britain) 1877

Displacement	40 tons
Length	90 feet
Engines	2,850 hp; triple expansion
Speed	19 knots

First of a new generation of enlarged British torpedo boats, built for the high seas.

Cruiser TAKACHIKO
(Japan) 1884

Displacement	3,650 tons
Length	300 feet
Beam	46 feet
Draught	18 feet 6 inches
Armament	2 × 10·3 inch guns
	6 × 5·9 inch guns
	2 × 6 pounder guns
	10 × 1 pounder guns
	4 × 14 inch torpedo tubes
Engines	7,000 hp; reciprocating
Speed	18·5 knots

Typical of the next generation of protected cruisers, she combined high speed with greater fighting power.

Cruiser DUPUY DE LOME
(France) 1888

Displacement	6,300 tons
Length	352 feet
Beam	46 feet 8 inches
Draught	18 feet 10 inches
Armament	2 × 7·6 inch guns
	6 × 6·4 inch guns
	6 × 5·5 inch guns
Main armour	4 inch belt
Speed	20 knots

A fast, well armed and protected cruiser built to give the French a more powerful type of commerce-raider.

Cruiser MINOTAUR

(Britain) 1906

Class	Minotaur (3 built)
Displacement	14,600 tons
Length	519 feet
Beam	74 feet 6 inches
Draught	26 feet
Armament	4×9·2 inch guns
	10×7·5 inch guns
	16×12 pounders
	5×18 inch torpedo tubes
Main armour	6 to 3 inch belt
Engines	27,000 hp; triple expansion
Speed	23 knots

Typical of British armoured cruisers in the first decade of the 20th century, when increasing emphasis was given to offensive power.

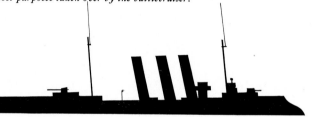

Light cruiser BREMEN

(Germany) 1903

Displacement	3,250 tons (normal)
Length	341 feet (waterline)
Beam	43 feet 6 inches
Draught	17 feet 6 inches
Armament	10×4·1 inch guns
	10×1 pounder guns
	4×18 inch torpedo tubes
Engines	11,000 hp; triple expansion
Speed	23 knots

First of a new type of cruiser built for reconnaissance work; the offensive role of armoured cruisers was for most purposes taken over by the battlecruiser.

Submarine A-1

(Britain) 1904

Displacement	165 tons (surface)
Length	99 feet
Beam	12 feet 9 inches
Armament	2×18 inch torpedo tubes
Motive power	450/80 hp; petrol (surface)
	electric (diving)
Speed	11 knots (surface)
	7 knots (submerged)

First British version of the American Holland submarine; the latter was the prototype for most of the world's navies.

Seaplane carrier LE FOUDRE

(France) 1892

Displacement	6,086 tons
Length	374 feet
Beam	52 feet
Draught	25 feet
Armament	8×4 inch guns
	4×9 pounder guns
	2×3 pounder guns
Engines	11,930 hp
Speed	19·6 knots

A converted depot ship, in 1912 she became the first seaplane carrier to be commissioned and so meet the need for a vessel capable of operating aircraft. In World War I landings on the surface of the sea remained the only means of recovery.

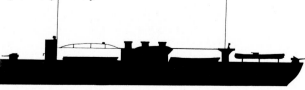

Aircraft carrier ARGUS

(Britain) 1917

Displacement	14,000 tons
Length	560 feet
Beam	68 feet
Draught	21 feet
Armament (first)	6×4 inch guns
Carrier capacity	20 aircraft
Engines	20,000 hp; triple expansion
Speed	20 knots

The prototype aircraft carrier with a continuous free deck; completed too late for action in World War I.

Battleship NAGATO

(Japan) 1917

Displacement	32,720 tons (standard)
Length	661 feet
Beam	95 feet
Draught	30 feet
Armament	8×16 inch guns
	20×5·5 inch guns
	4×3 inch guns
	8×21 inch torpedo tubes
Main armour	12 to 4 inch belt
Engines	80,000 hp; turbines
Speed	27 knots

Most powerful ship in the world when completed in 1920; later refitted in 1924 and rebuilt between 1934 and 1936.

Battlecruiser HOOD

(Britain) 1918

Displacement	41,200 tons
Length	860 feet
Beam	104 feet
Draught	28 feet 6 inches
Armament	8×15 inch guns
	12×5·5 inch guns
	4×4 inch AA guns
	4×3 pounders
	6×21 inch torpedo tubes
Main armour	12 to 5 inch belt
Engines	144,000 hp; turbines
Speed	31 knots

World's heaviest warship for most of her active lifetime (1920–41), she nevertheless suffered from inadequate armour protection.

Battlecruiser VITTORIO VENETO

(Italy) 1937

Displacement	35,000 tons (standard)
Length	754 feet
Beam	106 feet 6 inches
Draught	30 feet 6 inches
Armament	9×15 inch guns
	12×6 inch guns
	12×3·5 inch AA guns
	3 aircraft
Main armour	12 to 9 inch belt
Engines	130,000 hp; geared turbines
Speed	30 knots

A well armed ship that typified the Italian preference for speed before protection.

Battleship WASHINGTON
(USA) 1938

Class	Washington (6 built)
Displacement	35,000 tons
Length	729 feet
Beam	108 feet
Draught	26 feet 8 inches
Armament	9 × 16 inch guns
	20 × 5 inch DP guns
	4 aircraft (with 2 catapults)
Main armour	18 to 4 inch belt
Engines	121,000 hp; geared turbines
Speed	27 knots

First of an impressive class of capital ships that carried nine 16-inch guns.

Battleship YAMATO
(Japan) 1937

Displacement	64,000 tons
Length	863 feet
Beam	127 feet
Draught	35 feet
Armament (first)	9 × 18·1 inch guns
	12 × 6·1 inch guns
	12 × 5 inch AA guns
	24 × 25 mm AA guns
	4 × 13 mm guns
	6 aircraft
Main armour	16 inch belt
Engines	150,000 hp; steam turbines
Speed	27 knots

This ship and her sister, the Musashi, were the greatest battleships ever built. Completed after Pearl Harbor (December 1941), they were, however, already obsolescent, made thus by the carrier and its aircraft.

Aircraft carrier LEXINGTON
(USA) 1921

Displacement	36,000 tons
Length	888 feet
Beam	105 feet
Draught	24 feet
Armament	8 × 5 inch guns
	12 × 5 inch AA guns
	4 × 6 pounder guns
Carrier capacity	72 aircraft (later 90)
Engines	180,000 hp; turbines
Speed	34 knots

Originally laid down as battlecruisers, she and the Saratoga were converted and became the world's largest carriers.

Fleet carrier WASP
(USA) 1936

Class	Essex
Displacement	27,100 tons
Length	820 feet
Beam	147 feet 6 inches
Draught	20 feet
Armament	12 × 5 inch guns
	40 × 40 mm AA guns
Carrier capacity	100 aircraft
Engines	turbines
Speed	32 knots

One of the Essex class ships that became the standard US fleet carrier of World War II.

Cruiser ASHIGARA

(Japan) 1925

Class	Ashigara (4 built)
Displacement	10,900 tons
Length	631 feet
Beam	57 feet
Draught	19 feet
Armament	10×7·9 inch guns
	6×4·7 inch guns
	12 torpedo tubes
	2 aircraft
Main armour	4 inch belt
Engines	130,000 hp; turbines
Speed	35 knots

First class of Japanese cruisers designed from the beginning to exceed Washington Treaty limitations (set at 10,000 tons for cruisers).

Cruiser BOISE

(USA) 1936

Class	Brooklyn (9 built)
Displacement	10,000 tons
Length	608 feet
Beam	62 feet
Draught	19 feet 6 inches
Armament	15×6 inch guns
	8×5 inch AA guns
	4×3 pounders
	5×1 pounders
	4 aircraft
Main armour	4 to 1½ inch sides
Engines	100,000 hp; geared turbines
Speed	33 knots

A Brooklyn class cruiser with seaplane catapult placed in the stern.

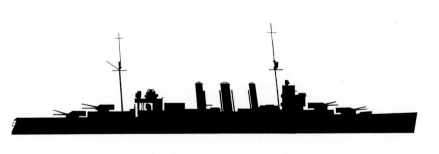

Cruiser KENT

(Britain) 1926

Class	County (11 built)
Displacement	9,750 tons
Length	630 feet
Beam	68 feet
Draught	16 feet
Armament	8×8 inch guns
	8×4 inch AA guns
	8×2 pounder AA guns
	8×21 inch torpedo tubes
Main armour	5 to 3 inch belt
Engines	80,000 hp; turbines
Speed	32 knots

County class cruiser built to maximum Washington Treaty limits and equipped with 8-inch guns.

Cruiser LEIPZIG

(Germany) 1929 (launch date)

Displacement	6,000 tons
Length	544 feet
Beam	53 feet 6 inches
Draught	15 feet 9 inches
Armament	9×5·9 inch guns
	6×3·5 inch AA guns
	8×3 pounder AA guns
	12×21 inch torpedo tubes
	2 aircraft (with catapult)
Main armour	4 to 3 inch sides
Engines	60,000 hp; geared turbines
Speed	32 knots

A powerful commerce-raider equipped with 5·9 inch guns – which were within the limits imposed by the 1919 Treaty of Versailles.

Pocket battleship DEUTSCHLAND

(Germany) 1929

Displacement	11,700 tons
Length	609 feet (overall)
Beam	67 feet 6 inches
Draught	21 feet 9 inches
Armament	6 × 11 inch guns
	8 × 5·9 inch guns
	6 × 4·1 inch AA guns
	8 × 3 pounder AA guns
	8 × 21 inch torpedo tubes
	2 aircraft (with catapult)
Main armour	4 inch belt
Engines	54,000 hp; diesel
Speed	27 knots

First of a new type of cruiser, which exceeded Treaty limits and belonged properly in the capital ship class.

Destroyer LANCE

(Britain) 1940

Class	L class (8 built)
Displacement	1,920 tons
Length	362 feet 6 inches
Beam	36 feet 6 inches
Draught	10 feet
Armament	6 × 4·7 inch DP guns
	8 × 4 inch AA guns
	4 × 2 pounder AA guns
	8 × 21 inch torpedo tubes
Engines	48,000 hp; geared turbines
Speed	36 knots

British L class destroyer, first to be fitted with dual purpose (DP) guns.

Destroyer CRAVEN

(USA) 1937 (launch date)

Class	Gridley (10 built, plus 12 of related Benham class)
Displacement	2,350 tons
Length	341 feet
Beam	35 feet
Draught	9 feet 9 inches
Armament	4 × 5 inch DP guns
	4 × 5 inch AA guns
	16 × 21 inch torpedo tubes
Engines	50,000 hp; geared turbines
Speed	40 knots

Long-range American destroyer of the Gridley class, the first to be able to refuel at sea.

Destroyer AKITSUKI

(Japan) 1940

Displacement	2,700 tons
Length	413 feet 6 inches
Beam	38 feet
Draught	13 feet 6 inches
Armament (first)	8 × 3·9 inch DP guns
	4 × 25 mm guns
	4 × 24 inch torpedo tubes
Engines	52,000 hp; turbines
Speed	33 knots

One of the Type B class of large destroyers which had the powerful 3·9-inch DP gun which outranged the contemporary US 5-inch gun.

Sloop BLACK SWAN

(Britain) 1939

Class	Black Swan (9 built, plus 22 modified versions)
Displacement	1,250 tons
Length	299 feet 6 inches
Beam	37 feet 6 inches
Draught	8 feet 6 inches
Armament	6 × 4 inch AA guns
	4 × 2 pounder AA guns
	4 × 0·5 inch AA guns
Engines	3,600 hp; turbines
Speed	19 knots

First of a class of sloops which carried out vital escort work in the North Atlantic.

Submarine TYPE VII-B

(Germany)

Displacement	753 tons
Length	218 feet
Beam	20 feet
Draught	15 feet 6 inches
Armament	1 × 3·5 inch gun
	1 × 20 mm AA gun
	5 × 21 inch torpedo tubes with 12 torpedoes
	or 14 mines
Speed	17·25 knots (surface)
	8 knots (submerged)

Staple German submarine in the early part of the Battle of the Atlantic.

Submarine I 400

(Japan) 1943

Displacement	6,550 tons
Length	380 feet
Beam	39 feet
Draught	23 feet
Armament	1 × 5·5 inch gun
	10 × 25 mm guns
	8 × 21 inch torpedo tubes
	3 seaplanes
Engines	7,700/2,400 hp; diesel/electric
Speed	18·75 knots (surface)
	6·5 knots (submerged)

One of the Type STO submarines – the largest conventionally powered submarines ever built.

Landing craft infantry LCI-1

(USA)

Displacement	216 tons
Length	154 feet
Beam	23 feet
Engines	1,600 hp; diesel
Speed	15 knots

A new type of ship designed for amphibious operations in World War II.

Aircraft carrier FORRESTAL

(USA) 1952

Class	Forrestal (4 built to date)
Displacement	62,000 tons
Length	1,039 feet
Beam	152 feet
Draught	37 feet
Armament	Sea Sparrow missiles
	80 aircraft
Engines	280,000 hp; geared turbines
Speed	35 knots

First nuclear-powered carrier, from which source she derives great flexibility and high-speed endurance.

Aircraft carrier ENTERPRISE

(USA) 1958

Displacement	89,600 tons
Length	1,123 feet
Beam	133 feet
Draught	36 feet
Armament	Sea Sparrow missiles
	90+ aircraft
Main machinery	8 nuclear reactors with
	4 geared turbines (280,000 hp)
Speed	35 knots

Post-war carrier, the first American ship too large to use the Panama Canal.

Fast patrol boat OSA

(USSR) c.1959

Class	Osa (approx. 125 built)
Displacement	165 tons
Length	128 feet
Beam	25 feet
Draught	6 feet
Armament	Styx missiles
	4 × 30 mm guns
Engines	13,000 hp; diesel
Speed	32 knots

Soviet class of light missile-armed ship, one of which sank the Israeli destroyer Eilat *with a* Styx *missile in the 1967 war.*

Submarine GEORGE WASHINGTON

(USA) 1959

Class	George Washington (5 built to date)
Displacement	5,900 tons
Length	382 feet
Beam	33 feet
Draught	29 feet
Armament	16 Polaris missiles
	6 × 21 inch torpedo tubes
Main machinery	1 nuclear reactor
	1 geared turbine (15,000 hp)

First submarine to fire a nuclear missile from beneath the surface of the sea.

2 : Missiles of the World's Navies A Selective Survey

Group 1 Strategic Missiles

POLARIS

(USA) 1960

Underwater-to-surface or surface-to-surface ballistic missile. In service of USA.

Length	31 feet 0 inches
Diameter	4 feet 6 inches
Weight	35,000 pounds
Speed	6,600 mph
Range	2,875 miles
Warhead	thermonuclear

SSN-4 SARK

(USSR) c.1961

Underwater-to-surface or surface-to-surface missile. In service of USSR.

Length	48 feet 0 inches
Diameter	5 feet 9 inches
Weight and performance	not known
Warhead	nuclear

POSEIDON

(USA) 1970

Underwater-to-surface or surface-to-surface ballistic missile. In service of USA.

Length	34 feet 0 inches
Diameter	6 feet 2 inches
Weight	65,000 pounds
Range	2,875 miles
Warhead	thermonuclear

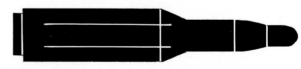

SSN-5 SERB

(USSR) c.1963

Underwater-to-surface or surface-to-surface missile. In service of USSR.

Length	35 feet 1 inch
Diameter	4 feet 10 inches
Weight and speed	not known
Range	750 miles
Warhead	nuclear or thermonuclear

SSN-6 SAWFLY

(USSR) *c.*1970

Underwater-to-surface or surface-to-surface missile.
In service of USSR.

Length	42 feet 0 inches
Diameter	5 feet 6 inches
Weight and speed	not known
Range	1,750 miles
Warhead	nuclear or thermonuclear

MSBS

(France)

Submarine-launched ballistic missile. In service of
France.

Length	34 feet 2 inches
Diameter	5 feet 0 inches
Weight	39,700 pounds
Range and speed	secret
Warhead	nuclear (500 kilotons)

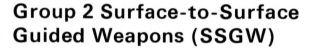

Group 2 Surface-to-Surface Guided Weapons (SSGW)

EXOCET

(France) 1971

Surface-to-surface tactical missile. In service of
France, Peru, Britain.

Length	16 feet 9 inches
Diameter	1 foot 3 inches
Weight	1,550 pounds
Speed	Mach 1
Range	23 miles
Warhead	high explosive (220 pounds)

OTOMAT

(Italy) 1970

Surface-to-surface tactical missile. In service of Italy.

Length	15 foot 8 inches
Diameter	1 foot 5 inches
Weight	1,530 pounds
Speed	Mach 0·8
Range	40 miles
Warhead	semi-armour-piercing (450 pounds)

GABRIEL

(Israel) 1970

Surface-to-surface missile. In service of Israel.

Length	11 feet 0 inches
Diameter	1 foot 0 inches
Weight	880 pounds
Speed	Mach 0·7
Range	12 miles
Warhead	high explosive (330 pounds)

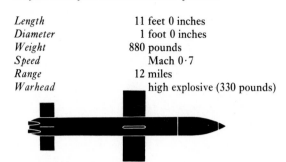

VOLCANO

(Italy) 1969

Surface-to-surface missile, also known as Sea Killer
Mark 2. In service of Italy.

Length	15 feet 4 inches
Diameter	8 inches
Weight	530 pounds
Speed	Mach 1
Range	5·6 miles
Warhead	semi-armour-piercing high explosive

PENGUIN

(Norway) 1970

Surface-to-surface tactical missile. In service of
Norway.

Length	10 feet 0 inches
Diameter	1 foot 0 inches
Weight	72 pounds
Speed	Mach 0·7
Range	18 miles
Warhead	high explosive (275 pounds)

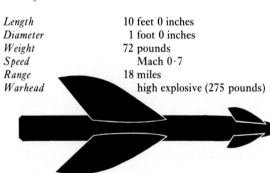

RBO8A

(Sweden) 1968

Surface-to-surface missile. In service of Sweden.

Length	18 feet 9 inches
Diameter	2 feet 2 inches
Weight	1,985 pounds
Speed and range	secret
Warhead	high explosive

SS-12

(France) 1965

Surface-to-air tactical missile. In service of France.

Length	6 feet 3 inches
Diameter	7 inches
Weight	165 pounds
Speed	425 mph
Range	19,650 feet (3·7 miles)
Warhead	armour-piercing

Group 3 Cruise Missiles

SSN-3 SHADDOCK

(USSR) 1970

Surface-to-surface cruise missile. In service of USSR.

Length	36 feet 0 inches (approx.)
Diameter and weight	not known
Speed	600 mph (approx.)
Range	400 miles (approx.)
Warhead	nuclear or conventional

Group 4 Surface-to-Air Guided Weapons (SAGW)

SEA CAT

(Britain) 1962

Surface-to-air and surface-to-surface missile for short-range work. In service of Britain, Australia, New Zealand, Sweden, Netherlands, and some South American countries.

Length	4 feet 11 inches
Diameter	7 inches
Weight	150 pounds
Speed	secret
Range	2·2 miles
Warhead	high explosive

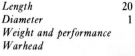

SEA SLUG

(Britain) 1967

Surface-to-air and surface-to-surface missile. In service of Britain.

Length	20 feet 0 inches
Diameter	1 foot 10 inches
Weight and performance	secret
Warhead	high explosive

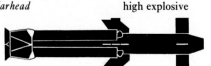

STANDARD RIM-66A

(USA) 1970

Supersonic surface-to-air missile. In service of USA.

Length	15 feet 3 inches
Diameter	1 foot 0 inches
Weight	1,300 pounds
Speed	Mach 1+
Range	15 miles
Warhead	high explosive

GOA

(USSR) 1970

Surface-to-air short-range missile. In service of USSR.

Length	19 feet 5 inches
Diameter	1 foot 8 inches
Weight and speed	not known
Range	15 miles (approx.)
Warhead	high explosive

SLAM

(Britain) 1970

Ship-launched missile system still under development and consisting of a cluster of six Blowpipe missiles launched from a common mounting. The details for the Blowpipe missile are:

Length	4 feet 6 inches
Diameter	4 inches
Weight and speed	secret
Range	2 miles
Warhead	high explosive (5 pounds)

SEA DART

(Britain) 1965

Surface-to-air and surface-to-surface missile. In service of Britain, Argentina.

Length	14 feet 3 inches
Diameter	1 foot 5 inches
Weight	1,210 pounds
Speed	secret
Range	20 miles
Warhead	high explosive

INDEX

Page numbers in *italics* refer to captions

ACKNOWLEDGEMENTS

The publishers would like to thank the following individuals and organisations for their kind permission to reproduce the pictures in this book:
Camera Press Ltd 72, 89 right Fox Photos 33 above, 66 left, 68–69 above, 113 above right General Dynamics 115 above Michael Holford 23 above Michael Holford/ National Gallery 14–15 Annie Horton 9 inset, 17 above, 19 above, 23 centre, 23 below, 24 above left, 25 Robert Hunt Library 4–5, 48 below, 60–61 below, 63 right, 68 left, 69 above right, 70 above left, 70–71 above, 71 inset, 73, 78 above right, 79 above, 79 below right, 81 below, 84–85 above, 88 above, 88 below, 97 above, 99 above left, 99 above right, 101 above, 104, 105 above, 105 below, 108–109 Illustrated London News 21 above Imperial War Museum 17 below, 24 below, 35 above, 36 below, 37, 38–39, 40 above, 40 below, 41 above left, 41 below, 42 above, 42 below, 43, 46–47 below, 47 above left, 47 below right, 49 above, 49 centre, 50 below, 50–51 above, 51 above right, 51 below, 52 above, 52–53 below, 55 above, 56, 57, 58 above left, 58–59 above, 59 above, 62 above, 62 below left, 62–63 above, 62–63 centre, 66 right, 67 above, 67 below, 67 centre, 76–77 below, 78 below, 79 below left, 81 above, 92 above, 92 below, 92–93 below, 96 above, 96–97 below, 98–99, 100 above Keystone 65 below, 69 below, 84 below, 103 right, 110–111 below, 112–113, 116, 120 above, 124–125 below Michael Leitch 26–27 below, 27 above, 27 centre Mansell Collection 13 above right, 16–17 above, 36 above Ministry of Defence 1, 6, 117 centre, 120 centre, 120 below, 121, 123 below Ministry of Defence/Royal Navy 114, 115 centre National Maritime Museum 10 below, 10–11 above, 12, 13 above left, 13 below, 15 inset, 28–29, 34–35, 35 centre, 35 below National Maritime Museum/Michael Holford 22 Novosti Press Agency 32, 33 below, 117 above, 117 below, 126 Popperfoto 45, 54–55 below, 58–59 below, 62–63 below, 64, 65 above, 70–71 below, 77 above, 84 above, 90 below left, 90 below right, 91 above, 91 below left, 91 below right, 100 below, 101 below, 102–103, 111 above, 124 above, 128–129 Science Museum 8–9, 9 above, 11 below Spectrum 118–119 below, 119 above U.S. National Archives 20–21 below, 29 above, 34, 78 above left U.S. Navy, Office of Information 18–19, 61 above, 108 inset, 113 centre right, 123 above, endpapers Vickers 123 below Derrick E. Witty 24 above right